Bless
my
Soul

Bless my Soul

A "Soul"-ution for All!

by Suzanne Salas

BONNEVILLE BOOKS™

Springville, Utah

ISBN: 1-55517-627-5
e.2

Published by Bonneville Books
Imprint of Cedar Fort Inc.
www.cedarfort.com

Distributed by:

Typeset by Kristin Nelson
Cover design by Nicole Cunningham
Cover design © 2002 by Lyle Mortimer

Printed in the United States of America
10 9 8 7 6 5 4 3 2 1

Printed on acid-free paper

Library of Congress Cataloging-in-Publication Data

Salas, Suzanne, 1946-
  Bless my soul : a "soul"-ution for all! / by Suzanne Salas.
    p. cm.
Includes bibliographical references.
  ISBN 1-55517-627-5 (pbk. : alk. paper)
  1. Spiritual life--Miscellanea. I. Title.

BF1999 .S3122 2003
299'.93--dc21
                        2002015283

This book is dedicated
to you.

Everyone is in a hurry in life to LIVE,
but no one is in a rush to get to Heaven.

Search no more. This is the bottom line book.
We're all going somewhere when our body wears out.

All
roads
lead
to
Home.

Wherever you are right now, whomever you are with,
what you think and feel are absolutely perfect.
You are where you have chosen to be and where you belong.

Foreword

You will live forever. You will not go to hell. And those who have "done you wrong" will get what they deserve. The person you want to love you will love you, eventually. There is an alternative to suicide, though neither is recommended. And sex after death is good. All knowledge is available to you. No one judges you. And thoughts are real things. You are God. Ghosts, aliens, black holes, the Bermuda triangle, the Abominable Snowman, and the Devil are real. So are Angels and the light at the end of the tunnel. The person you hate will go away, though maybe not easily. Not everyone agrees—even in Heaven. And tomorrow is another day. The family you have, you chose. You also chose your nose, height, feet, eye, and hair color. You have another half somewhere. The Universe is unlimited, which means all abundance and money is yours and even due you. You are forgiven. And all beauty and music are yours. You are energy. If you can read this book you can understand everything, such as: Who am I? Why am I here? Where am I going?

This book is not a guide, plan, or how-to book; it is simply one of many books available to you that provides information, love, and courage to be on your way. There are many tools on Earth to help you, of which this is just one. This does not include all that is available from family, friends, co-workers, children, church, the Internet, astrology, psychiatrists, magnets, acupuncture, mountain-sitting in Tibet, your MD, beautician, barber, numerologist, chiropractor, Tai-chi, tarot, yoga, meditation, the Bible, guides, crystals, herbal teas, body building, multivitamins, and whatnot. All of these tools are good, but the best tool to help you live this life is the perfect, imaginative-seeking you.

Actually, you already have all the answers. You've always known the answers. It's just that you've forgotten them because you're busy living and loving, working and playing. It's wonderful that you are about your life and doing as you wish. After all, you are free and choices are yours to make or, if you don't like the choice, to remake as you change your mind! Isn't it great?

All is just as it should be. There is no mystery, for truth is simple. The journey of living in a body on Earth is exciting and challenging. How brave and incredible you are to come on this personal and humanitarian mission. Look around at all who have joined you and signed up to help you, as you signed up to help them.

There are no weird words, hard concepts, or bizarre revelations in this book, so just flow along and enjoy it. Take it or leave it. You're allowed. It's about you, your dreams, love life, and hopes. It's about your job, sex life, daydreams, and nightmares. This book will talk about great joy, awful physical pain, betrayal, passionate love, rejection, fear, laughter, the Universe, the energy you are, and the makeup of our experience on Earth that moves you. It will also go into your physical body, your thinking mind, your emotions, your personality, and the fuel that keeps this fine machine going, the energy of your spirit and soul.

It's not hard. In fact, it's fun to explore who you are. You are your favorite topic. Everyone loves to gossip about the next person. So we will explore him or her, too. Often, we want to know, "Why is this person in my life?" and "Why does he do this or that?" We even say, "If I were her, I'd do such and such." Well, we each have good ideas and an absolute right to them. The trick, though, is how we use what we know. Are you responsible for your thoughts and actions? Do you have a plan or are you just hanging out? Either is okay, of course. Some people are here to hang out and others are on a great mission within the mission of living on Earth. Sort of like the astronauts are on a mission together, but one in the group may have a special mission to study and explore gravity's effect on ladybugs! The others are along for the ride. They all have important jobs, but aren't focused on just one big goal.

Look at any family. There are members who mosey through life, do fine, work every day, and raise a nice family; however, there may be one member who is known to the world for something special he or she has done. We are all breathing the same air, taking up space, and having our own experiences. No one is more special or less important than the other; we are all on a journey of human life and working together. We each use our energy in a different way. There is no right or wrong. Come; let us explore together.

Every word in this book has been written before. Every thought has been thought and every action has been acted, reacted, and acted again. In fact, the cast is the same on this stage of life on Earth. As the saying goes, "nothing is new under the sun." Your purpose for living is not as complex as you think. That's the good news. Better yet, there is no bad news! These pages will unfold before you and may speak to you—the most important person on Earth—in a way that will unlock your memory so that you realize why you are here in this now. Remember, all knowledge is yours, and is available to you. The tricky part is getting to it and how you choose to use it after you have it. The beautiful thing is that you can learn and change anything. Now this is powerful stuff! To begin, however, a certain attitude must be adopted, an attitude that says, "I am flexible; I am open to new things and all things are possible." See, you've heard that last phrase before.

No matter how difficult or complex your life is because of the people you've chosen to be around, no matter how tough your job is, or how mad, angry, hurt or disappointed you are, take heart this moment and know that you are doing the very best you can do. This seems impossible and even weird, but it's true. As the moment changes, circumstances change, and as circumstances change, you change. So, whatever your pain or joy, as you read this, you will change, must change, this is a law of energy. It does not matter if you are male, female, young, old, well, sick, fat, thin, alone, witty, weird, and a page of other adjectives. You are first, last, and always, ENERGY.

There is no time. You are timeless and no matter how you think and feel about yourself or how others perceive you, you are perfect and eternal. Cool, huh? Indeed, it is. Deep down you know it. The very core of you knows this to be as true as you are holding this book, this minute. Think for a moment. What do you believe? If the words of this book sit well with you in your gut and mind, if it feels right, then continue. Otherwise, put the book down and do not be disturbed. You are where you belong. Pass the book to another, throw it out, or go get your money back! However, just as you want to be respected for your beliefs, respect all others in theirs.

Table of Contents

Chapter 1

Hello Dearest

Hello Dearest:

I am your Angel. You know that everyone has an Angel, don't you? Everyone who picked up this book is from the same source, yet each of you is uniquely different and wonderful, and has your own Angel. We Angels got together and decided I'd be the writer to tell you all about yourself. So it has been given to me, after many brainstorming sessions, to put it down on paper.

You hear people say these days that "children don't come with instructions." Well, they actually do. You already know this, of course, because you have been a child before and knew how you wished to be loved and handled. It takes both: handling until you think you'll go crazy, and love galore. It also means you have to be patient and giving, to accept and nurture a soul as it begins its travels here on Earth.

Let's back up to why I am telling you all this. You are a very important part of me. As you treasure your arms, legs, eyes, hearing, hair, teeth, and taste buds, I treasure you. As these things are a vital part of you, you are very much a vital part of me. So, it stands to reason that I wish to protect important parts of me just as you protect your own limbs. I am your Angel. I deeply care that you understand why you are in a physical body on the Earth, why you live with whom you do, and where and why. And if you and I know why, then we all do better; we grow better, love better, and live better. It's this simple. Really. Would your very own Angel lie to you? Never.

1

You are very brave to pick up this book. You are searching for answers and reasons, which is wonderful. This is a part of your blooming and I will be with you the entire way on every page. Life is fun, the trip is fun, and the challenges, though very hard sometimes, are very purposeful.

Whenever taking new steps, there need to be some guidelines and this book is no different. There are three easy guidelines, and you know each of them. The first rule is that no matter how old you are, now is the time to open your mind and be flexible. After all, you picked up this book to take a new thinking adventure. I'm an easy-read writer.

The second rule to keep in that open mind of yours is the fact that everything is possible, and that you have NO limitations. This is good stuff, and absolutely true. Sure, you may be reading this in a prison, surrounded by high walls, a mom whose dishes are piling up in the kitchen, a teen with zits and no friends—or so you think, or a man with no clue as to where you are going next, but you really, really have NO limitations. Of course, I will explain as we go, so hang in there. Okay. Your mind is open. You are thinking flexibly and the possibilities are limitless.

You have already believed this, done this, and had these thoughts. It's what got you to this place in time. You are a miracle of your own thoughts, desires, and wishes. You're a pretty terrific and remarkable being.

Delete now from your thinking your own politics, finances, love life, and religion, or lack thereof. Using the terms of the day, let's "populate" the field of your thoughts with some new ones. Most of you use a computer as a tool for work or fun and do this every day, counting on and looking forward to "something new" on your screen. Well, this book is a new "program" or "new data" so to speak. For those of you, my dearest, who haven't touched a computer and don't intend to, cheer up. You can imagine the blank pages of a newspaper before it goes through the presses to imprint on them "the news." In either case, as with all cases, you are the writer of the program, or the news; it's all yours. What do you want to read about yourself? Begin to think it. Begin to write it.

No matter what your age is, as you read my words, you have a mind that is set actively and strongly in place. As you read this story about what got you here, you want to learn something NEW, right? Well, to make room for the new, one has to shove out the old. As on a computer, information doesn't always fit, so you need more space to hold it. In a newspaper, the same stories aren't repeated day after day, some stories are let go, to make room for new ideas.

So, here you go on your thinking adventure with a flexible, open, and limitless mind. This will be fun. If you don't think so, then you have a choice, which is the third rule for this trip: know that at all times, no matter what, *you have a choice!* What you create, you can "un-create." Everything is always up to you.

I realize that this is a mind stretcher. Some of you are in terrible circumstances, and may ask how you can possibly "un-create" the ugly, unwanted, painful, and downright difficult situations and people in your life. Well, during this personal journey, you will see, you will feel, and you will know the choices that surround you.

Remember, you have to put aside the politics, religions, job trials, and love quests to think anew. These ideas, these words, and this history that I give to you are all yours. In this time now it must sit "right" with you. If it does not, please go forward and do your best. I know you will. Not everyone is meant to take the same journey at the same time.

You are flowing, as you should. I must tell you now how very honored I am to be your Angel. I see you sparkling, I hold your heart, I catch your tears, I measure your steps, I bless each effort, and I rejoice with you in your beautiful, ongoing journey to perfect yourself. You are so wonderful, and I am so blessed to know you. I learn from you, too, for we have an even flow of love between us. I am always here, loving you. *Remember this: No matter who you are, where you are, or what you are; I am here loving you.* Hold this thought deeply to your heart and mark this page so you can return to it often to re-read it and reassure yourself. Love is a perfected expression, and you have mine. You got it? We are ONE and the same, and I love you. We may be at different places, but we are together in sharing the journey of the marvels of our OWN creations.

I choose now to talk to you in these written words, and you choose to read them. The exchange is happening. I write and you read. You think and read some more. New ideas, new thoughts, replace old ones. You use your new thoughts to understand who you are, where you are, and why. You share these ideas either by example or by actively talking with those around you. You change the computer program, the newspaper headlines. New news is a good thing; it's what we want and what we look forward to. Are you with me? Are you ready? My arms are around you; I am hugging you. You are good and I adore you.

I know what you most want to know about: Money and Love. It is the stuff of your physical life. Both make your world go around. You think, "How can I get both? I need both. I want both." What you want is comfort, and both create comfort. Every single day, as you awaken, your life is about making money, making love, and struggling to make life easier. You don't get up, look in the mirror, and say to yourself, "How can I be truly miserable and inconvenienced today? How can I get sick, hurt someone, wreck my car, and throw my money away?" Quite the contrary. You are constantly trying to fix things, pay for stuff, and get the guy or gal to notice and love you. You want to do, think, act, and be as you wish.

In all of the details of these struggles lay your creation of circumstances and choices. It is the "stuff" of the Earth-school curriculum, where everyone is in a different grade ranging from preschool to Ph.D. to ancient wise guy! It's really neat and you are a good student no matter what class you are in or moving to. In fact, you are a winner just by showing up for the class, which is this life you're living on Earth. As in all things, some of you learn more quickly than others, and some need to repeat a grade. However, everyone is going to graduate someday.

In all school programs, you study history. Well, you have a very interesting one; let me tell you about it. Picture a drop of water. This is you. Now picture two more drops, these are your parents. Add more drops, and see these as your siblings, family, and friends. At this point, your water drops may fill up a teaspoon. Now add your neighbors and your co-workers; add a drop for each person in your town, county, and state. Wow! Now you have a good sized puddle. Keep going. Add a drop for each person in the whole country, and then throw in a drop for each person in Canada and Mexico. Do you have a pond? Do you remember learning the seven continents? Well, add a drop of water for each person on each of them and all the islands and ships at sea! Look closely for the hermits and folks hiding out and tribes in the jungles. Add a drop for each of them. Maybe you have created a lake representing "everyone." For good measure, let's throw in all living things; add all the plants, animals, and bugs on Earth. We are making an ocean of droplets. We've got everyone and everything on Earth "pooled" together. But wait, there's more; more we can't see, feel or imagine, even in space and galaxies. This is pretty big, but to be safe, add another "ocean" of drops to represent "everyone."

Where are you? You are flowing in this beautiful, moving, waving, changing ocean. Without the drop that is YOU, this ocean would not be complete; it would not be the All. Every drop is essential to complete this picture.

Now, in your great imagination, turn these gazillion drops into little, but strong lights! Wow, don't blind yourself now! Isn't this a staggeringly bright, beautiful, and even glaring sight? Well, you are one of these brilliant, glowing lights. Now light is energy and energy cannot be destroyed; it can, however, be changed into different forms. This ocean of light is the All, and you are a "light spark" in the All. The All is what we call God. Thus, God is All and All is God, which means that as a part of the All, you are God!

Take a minute, or two, or three to think about this. It may hurt your brain a little, but not for long. Let the news sink in of just how important, powerful, and wonderful you are. Yes, you are God, which leads—here we go now—to the fact that so is everyone else!

In the beginning . . . well, actually, there was no beginning, just as there is no end. It's hard to imagine this, for it's a pretty heady thought that all things are eternal, but it's true. In different forms and in different ways, you use your choices and your very own ideas to create and recreate the new, improved you. Which brings us back to the top-of-the-line thought that, "You are God."

Bear with me now, love. Replace the old picture you have of an all-powerful being sitting on a throne amidst the clouds, pointing his finger at creation. Zap, it snows! Zap, she dies. Zap, my husband drinks too much. Zap, the crop died. Zap, the rain forest is destroyed. Zap, you are black, white, green, yellow, or pink. Zap. You are gorgeous, fat, sweet, or mean. Zap, your house is crushed in a mudslide. Zap, you have cancer. Stop asking, "Oh, how can God let this happen?" He doesn't, because he isn't! Remember, you are God. You are a part of the All, as is your fellow man. You are all energy, and you make the decisions. You call the shots, from whom your parents are, to where you live, how you look, what you do, why you do it, and how you die. Yes, you, you, you! You got it?

So, on one hand, isn't it amazing that all you sparks of light get along as well as you do, what with all the choices, plans, and ideas that exist from second to second? On the other hand, wouldn't the "project" flow much better if all your fellow "light" brothers and sisters realized their own power and influence, and truly, truly saw one another as a fellow God?

Take a break. Think on this. It is a lot to put on the front page of your newspaper or store on your hard drive. Take a deep breath and suck in this realization. You really have always known this. You've just forgotten, which is why I am writing you. I am your Angel, reminding you of who you are. Isn't this neat stuff? Well, YOU are neat stuff, and then some.

REMEMBER . . .

- You have an Angel.
- Keep a free and open mind.
- Everything is possible. No limitations.
- You always have choices.
- You have the power to create and "un-create."
- Everyone will graduate from the Earth-school.
- You are light energy.
- Energy can't be destroyed.
- You are God. So is everyone else.

Chapter 2

Making Choices

You can't NOT create. What good does a barrel of gasoline do sitting on an island? It's energy contained. The gasoline is not yet poured into a car, airplane, tractor, or whatever, to make it go. With the gasoline, these vehicles can be moved to create something else: take the child to school, fly the Red Cross volunteer to a disaster site, plow the field. You are energy, like the gasoline; only in your case, you're a huge hunk of light powering the vehicle that is your physical body. Remember the All with its collection of lights? Energy is your fuel from the power source of the All. Everyone agreed to the same equal, creative rights. Whatever you can do with your energy, so can others. Being from the same unimaginable, massive light source, each light has the same power and freewill to create in any way it wishes. This is what is called a divine right: the divine right of freewill.

Freewill to Make Choices. These words in your vocabulary are among the most powerful in the Universe! Think of it. With the right of your own freewill, you can make absolutely any choice you want to make, at any time, and anywhere, and so can everyone else! You can make good choices or bad choices. You have the choice to come, go, give, take, frown, smile, eat, cry, sit, or run. You even make the decision to be male or female, choose a skin color, and choose this planet, continent, and country. Every day you choose when to sleep, to dream, to love, and to hate. This is just the beginning of your freewill. You decide whether to have a life of ease, a life of struggle, or a little of both. You choose a short life or a long life. You choose to live in one place, fly to the moon, or travel the world. You can choose to sit all day or to journey to the North Pole.

It is your right to experience the same situation repeatedly or not. Of course, you may choose to never do anything. This, too, is a choice (but pretty hard to do). In the future, you may not even choose to be in human form as you are now. Some light energies, as is their right, have not. It is how you make and experience your choices that define the unique you! It is all okay. It is all creative. It is all freewill.

As with every group, there are rules; there have to be. You agreed on this, with all your fellow lights in the All, because with so many making choices and creating, as is your right, things could get out of hand. Now, you have to know the rules of the road before you drive a car, right? It also helps to know where you are going and how to get there. Of course, there are many ways to get to one place and many roads from which to choose, from the highway to the scenic route. There has to be order on the roads, though, because if there isn't, accidents happen. If you don't stop at the railroad crossing and neither does the train, then there is a mess, not to mention pain, inconvenience, and stuff to clean up before you can go on your way. It is the same with choices. You all also agreed that if you make a choice that causes pain, inconvenience, or a mess to your fellow man, then you are responsible for it and will fix it, correct it, clean it up, and even experience it yourself if need be, to make things right.

Now this is cool information to have. It is good to know who you are and where you stand in the very big picture. As I have said, you are quite remarkable and have already come a long, long way. Look around you. Everyone else is on the journey, too. Now, wouldn't it be just wonderful if every single person realized not only how neat you are, but also how neat he or she is? More importantly, wouldn't it be wonderful if you all recognized that each of you is on your own great adventure to create new experiences through your choices and to correct your not-so-great choices? Well, your fellow men and women are getting there, just as are you. Remember, you're each in a different place; after all, you didn't all start at the same time and some of you have made choices to leapfrog ahead. Of course, some of you have made awful choices over and over again, which has set you back, and your journey has slowed down because you've had to fix, correct, and pay back those you've affected. You all agreed that this is the right thing to do. So where are we with our open mind and new ideas? Let's see: you are God, who is responsible for your choices, and so is everyone else!

There is the right use of the energy "you" and there is the misuse of the energy "you." When there is misuse, it must, in time, be re-created into right use. It's the rule. You all agreed. Well, of course—this makes sense. Let's say that Sam owes you money. Eventually, you will want it back. Or if Aunt Alice hurts your feelings, you'll want an apology. If the kids empty a feather pillow in the basement, it's only fair that they clean it up. Similarly, if you are in pain, you want it to go away. If your heart is sad, you want to be loved to feel better. With every good-bye, you want a hello. With every new face, you want a smile. With every dream and life, you want a happy ending. This is balance. You put forth your energy to attain balance for yourself as well as for your loved one's balance. When you are angry, you are out of balance. If you are sad, sick, nasty, or experiencing anything extreme, you are out of balance. So it is with the Universe you live in, your home planet, and all the plant and animal life around you. Remember, they too are creative energy and part of the All. And like you, have creative freewill and responsibility for it.

Open your flexible mind now. Make room for a new

thought. You helped create the Universe, the planet, every leaf, bug, beach, rock, hill, valley, and the rhythm in which it works and flows. Each and all began with a single, creative thought. What a think tank! What a fabulous, creative pool of ideas! What size! What color! How wonderful! Water, air, fire, diamonds, fleas, elephants, metals, and the big topper, the human body and all its workings inside and out! Unbelievable! Incredible! Fantastic! But true, all true. Yes, you and your light buddies in your early creative days created all of this through limitless imagination. From the single cell, to the color red, to sight, sound, and hairy heads—wow! There was no stopping you and there is no stopping you now. Or anyone else!

Oh my. By now, you have a new and truer picture of the incredible you. I'm impressed. What a birth story, what a history. And this is just the beginning. Think on these things. Talk about them with your friends. Hear what they think. Just remember, they are who and where they are by their choice. You are all growing, learning, and experiencing at your own pace. It is your nature to talk and share. You all get out of bed every day to hear the news, read the news, check your favorite web site, read e-mail, look at ads, and talk to your friends. When you ask, "What's new with you?" what you are really saying is: "What more have you learned and experienced?" "How are you using your energy?" "Are you balancing?" "What are you going to do about it?" "Have you a new idea?" "Can you fix it, make it, get it, or move it?"

Each time you ask these questions, you are taking in new ideas and shared experiences because you are all teachers of one another. You're in this adventure together, just as you actually chose the groups you are in. These groups can include family groups, work and social groups, even your neighborhood and country groups along with all the circumstances that go with them. You don't remember these choices because the brain you created can only hold so much information, just as the computer and newspaper has only so much space. But, you can go back to the archives to retrieve old news or check the files on stored disks. You can ask your grandparents what they remember and history can be retrieved.

This is my gift for you now, to retrieve your history from the beginning so that you have a clearer understanding of yourself in the present: the remarkable, loving you. I do this because I haven't forgotten that you are a part of me and that all of us, together, are one great big energy source of creative power. As your Angel, I am here to guide you and to show you some possible new choices in ways of thinking, acting, loving, and appreciating your life force and all the choices you've made up to this moment in time. Every second is new and energy can be altered any way you want it.

Let's flow on together now and unfold the marvels of you and your light friends' creations. Truth is not complicated. You create because you can. There are no secret motives, no fate or fortune or destiny or hand of a one "God-being" pushing you this way and that way. No one is making you do this or that, though at times it may seem so. All is choice. There are very few "always" and "nevers" in the entire history of energy, and when we get to the few there are, you will learn that they were created by popular opinion and agreement by everyone in the All.

Everything is energy, and it is how you accept it, use it, and move it around that matters. Remember, you can change it, but cannot destroy it. Likewise, you yourself are energy and cannot be destroyed. You can change forms, but you do not die. Your energy exists forever and ever, and so does everyone else's! This is your right. How, when, and where you use your energy is up to you, as you wish, as you choose. Now aren't you something? Of course you are!

I write these words to you with the highest love. My desire is for the two of us to keep searching together for the right use of our energy so that we may find the very best expression of who we are through thoughts, words, and actions. I am your guardian and guide. I am beside you, around you, and within you. We are one and All. It is my mission and choice in this "life expression" to remind you of where you come from and who you are. You will choose to use this information as you wish, but I want you to know, there are no secrets. Everything is yours, just as all knowledge is available to you. You've just forgotten. To remember everything would be a great burden. You could not live in the NOW and experience your choices with the distractions of all your memories. Learning is ongoing, as you are, and you will learn what you need to know when you are ready to understand it. Of course, this happens at a different pace for everyone, so others must not be judged. To judge would be a misuse of energy.

In pages to come, I will write more for you on this. For now, take another deep breath and in doing so, be positive and a bright light and say "yes" to the wonders of your creations.

REMEMBER . . .

- You are All Energy. You are God.
- Freewill to make choices.
- We create because we can.
- We are responsible for our energy use.
- Everything is energy.
- Truth is simple.
- Few "always" and "nevers."
- There are no secrets.
- Energy is endless.
- You are endless, and so is everyone else.

Chapter 3
In the Beginning

Let's go back to the All. Try to picture it. See it as the sun, though it's not really the sun, but for a picture to grasp the thought of energy, it's a good start. You know that the sun is hot, huge, and bright. You know its power to give light and heat. At night, we see and feel less heat from the sun and receive no light (unless you live close to the Poles). Okay, now multiply the size and intensity of the sun over and over again to the point of exhaustion. Now multiply it again. With this "picture" you have a start at imagining the All of energy. Next, you have to "put" it someplace since the human mind needs to label and categorize in order to understand a concept. Since our picture of the sun is not the All, let's give the place a name. The most well-known and best-understood name is Heaven. So, Heaven is Home, a birthplace, a starting point, and a place to which you want to return.

"Okay," you say, "how did we get from a light in the All, to here and now reading this book, in a complicated body on this planet Earth full of stuff?" Well, once upon a time (all good books begin this way), a single energy thought, "Let's experiment. Let's create." So over eons of time, all the lights in the All toyed around with making things, like the planet Earth and our solar system. Everything you created was thought out, designed, and planned. You thought about where it would be, how it would work, and how it would take its place with all the other lights of the SAME energy. All of this creating occurred over a span of time we cannot begin to imagine, but you did it

and really had fun doing it! Actually, you stil'   ᶜᵎ
   Most in the All would agree that the creₐ
Earth was a top-notch job. It is considered a reₐ
creating it, you all envisioned being on it in your "spacₑ .
your human body. And what else would you need to visit youɪ
creation? You planned ahead very well and put on the Earth all
the plants, minerals, animals, gases, water, soils, and—a really
great idea—gravity, that you would need during your visit.

   Once you had a place to go, you first experimented in the
simplest way. A thought is energy, and energy is real; therefore,
thoughts are real things. So, being as smart as you are, you first
explored this new place in thought. Some light energy went
farther than others and found a plant form they liked, and then
experimented with being in this energy form. Then, animals
were designed and some lights experienced this life form. The
animal life form was a good design challenge and led to the
creation of a vast array of animal species. The ape is an early
form you made, which was perfected over time. This experi-
mentation with different animal body types led to early forms
of man. Remember though, you are first, last, and always pure
energy, for energy is the juice and fuel of life. More importantly, all energy is good energy; it is how you choose to use it
that can alter it into a misuse of energy.

   Do you have the picture? The big All, jam-packed with
lights full of creative energy ready to try something new. There
you are, a part of the All, and there is this planet sitting pretty,
out there in flowing space. A long time ago, some of you said,
"Well, I'm going to make a body form and put my energy in it
and see what it is like." And just as "Heaven" became a name
for the All from which all energy flows, the energy in your
human body became known as the "soul."

   Let's create another picture by looking at the family group.
Imagine your parents. Place them at the core of your family

roup. Now, picture yourself and all of your siblings around your mom and dad. When you are a young one, you are at home being nurtured by the energy of your parents. Little by little, though, you expand your own energy and don't need as much from them. After a while, you are going out of your home to learn, experiment, and grow; yet, even when you are grown up and out on your own, you still call Mom and Dad for input, advice, help, and support. Their energy of love and help is always there. Your parents chose to be your source, providers, and guides, just as you chose to be their child. Now, maybe one of your brothers chooses to stay home. Well, that's his choice. Maybe your sister goes far away and only occasionally calls home or visits. Maybe you live in the same town and visit Mom and Dad once a week and call them frequently.

Each soul is connected to the All at home in Heaven, as the children in the family example are to the mom and dad. You grow up, making a choice to go out and experience life. You—the soul—has the ever-loving and everlasting energy flowing to you from the All. Remember, you can have help anytime you want it and it will be freely and lovingly supplied because it is yours. No matter where you go, the fuel you need is there to constantly supply you. You also have fellow soul helpers in many forms of energy to rely on, both in Heaven and out in the world. At home in the family group, besides your parents, you have grandparents, aunts, uncles, cousins, and friends. In Heaven, there are energies that "know" you better than others and love you as you love them. As parents agree to help you in life on Earth, your "family" in the All agrees to help in your soul growth, as you choose to be in body form to learn and experience.

Now, isn't this just wonderful? What an adventure! And, just as all the children in a family don't leave home at the same time, neither do souls leave Heaven at the same time.

Therefore, each soul is at a different place in its growth and experience. Just as parents teach their children individually according to who they are and what they need, each soul has a different plan. Likewise, your "family" in the All doles out encouragement and guidance as you need it and as you ask for it.

I realize that the last example I gave you is the ideal situation on the planet Earth. Of course, you and I know that "family" groups are very different all over the world and some family situations are horrible and destructive. I realize this might be hard to hear, but the situation you are in is by choice. There are reasons for this. If this "family" core group does not work for you, use your creative gifts and think of one that does. Sometimes, job-related groups have a boss-employee situation where the company provides support to its employees to help them become more successful. Even one friend can be the source with which you can relate, someone who is always there to listen to you and give you love and help, and who will learn with you. Find a person or group that supports you. Everyone on Earth is a part of everyone at Home and both places are sources of love and help for you to see that you are far more than flesh, blood, and bone!

Just as your family and friends support you on Earth, the All energy at Home is full of souls helping one another do whatever they want to do! And when you are done with your visit and lessons and learning on Earth, you will go back Home, where you will be joyfully welcomed.

All knowledge is available to you as your soul evolves, and as you are ready to understand it. Just as a baby can't do algebra until other math skills are mastered, you don't understand your parents until you are a parent.

REMEMBER . . .

- Heaven/All Energy is God.
- The soul energy chooses to make choices.
- Thoughts are real things.
- All energy is good energy.
- Energy is the fuel of life.
- You are Soul Energy, first, last, and always.
- And so is everyone else!

Chapter 4

You Created Evolution

"Nothing is instantly ripened and nothing is suddenly great."
—Anonymous

Creation or evolution? How could there be one or the other? You created the growing and evolving of every life form from all energy. Some think it has to be one or the other: creation as the story of Adam and Eve, or evolution with cell mutation, survival of the fittest, changing form to become man.

Keep in mind that your brain is a physical mass that you created. It is a small computer in comparison to the mega, gargantuan, record keeping, order-observing mainframe in the All, which has NO boundaries; it is limitless, just as its possibilities are limitless.

You contain a part of your energy in your body, yet you have access to the All energy whenever you need it, simply by thinking a thought to pull it to you for your use. You create what you want by thinking it! Everyone else is doing this, too, so just think of all those thoughts out there flying around. Your brain is your personal computer and since everyone has one, all the thoughts are like the World Wide Web. You can tap into others' ideas by searching and thinking. You can "search" by knowing who you are and what you can do. Or, if the computer idea doesn't appeal to you, it would be like watching every news story on TV, hearing every radio news broadcast, and reading every newspaper. By asking, investigating, and thinking, you find what you want. This is why you often hear the same sayings and story themes repeated. Then a man argues, "It was MY idea first!" Well, maybe it was, but first "it" was a thought "out there" flying around and perhaps several people picked up on it.

But I am getting off the subject of creating evolution. You cleverly put a whole bunch of thoughts together and made your body. To make the body function, it needed an engine. So you built a pumping station, the heart, and a control booth, the brain, to make it move. Well, it wouldn't move until you put fuel in it, so you provided your own energy, that light which is a part of the All, and loaded the brain with it. You turned the switch on, being born on Earth, and voilá, a moving, walking, talking, thinking, and feeling being begins a great adventure. Your fuel of energy is constantly flowing to you from Home. It is always there for you to use as you wish until you decide to "take your light and go Home."

You put a time limit on the use of the machine of your body. Some short, some long, but most always by your choice. I say most always because sometimes, one soul making a choice gets in the way of another soul making a choice, which stops the body-machine from working and he or she goes Home early. There's no limit to your soul energy—it is constant. It's only the physical body that wears out.

Okay now. You've got the picture of you creating you. I am sure there are things about your physical body that you do not like and are thinking, "Never would I have given myself this nose!" Well, yes, you would and did, and you had your own good reason and choice to do so. So buck up and love whatever it is you created and get on with your adventure on Earth. Keep your mind open, go with the flow, and don't say "no" to anything until you've digested it a while.

You created time to keep everything in some order. It has taken lots of time to create the planet you live on and everything on it. It took you more time to design today's human body in which your soul energy resides. Life on Earth began with a thought, then a shadowy form. Gradually, it gained weight, or matter. Early on, there was a body form that was short, stocky, and hairy and several souls decided to put their energy in them and see what would happen. On the planet, they moved this body around in a place they called Lemuria somewhere in what we now know as the Pacific Ocean.

It was a fun experiment. The souls that chose this adventure were joined by other souls. It was new and every moment of every day was full of creating new things. The souls all interacted in new ways with one another because they were no longer just energy of thought, but energy of thought in a new form. So, obviously, there was more to consider. The energy was also CONTAINED now in a body form. However, these Lemurians remembered that what they were experiencing was an act of choice and creation. They were always aware of the source and the All. This is important to remember in this history of soul evolution and experiments in creation.

The Lemurians had a leader who stayed in connection with Home through meditation, and teachers who guided and directed them. They were thrilled with their wonderful creations. They didn't forget Home and they knew they were spirit first. They created and put their ideas into forms like plants and animals, and let them flow on their own.

About the same time, other souls thought they would experiment with a design of their own. This was sort of like GM vs. Ford, only it was not a competition. These souls chose another spot on the planet and called it Atlantis. Their body design was taller and they had orange-golden skin. They, too, were from the same All energy source and put their energy in a different body type. Other souls joined them and they really went to town creating a remarkable civilization. After all, they, too, had limitless possibilities in their power to create. For a while, the Lemurians traded with the Atlantians, but their lifestyle was more primitive than the Atlantians' and contact lessened over time.

Now, all the other lights of energy were at Home watching to see what would happen next! Many Atlantians were interested in how things worked on Earth since the planetary makeup and atmosphere were different from Home. They had created bigger and stronger bodies and were curious and intellectual. They came to think that the mind and the mental process were more important than their link with Home.

They built temples and had teachers who stayed in contact with Home through prayer and meditation. They were warned that they were playing with some of the natural rules that had been set up and agreed upon by All before beginning to create. They also were told by souls at Home that they were making mistakes and creating things difficult to control, which could cause damage to the planet and to them. This civilization and its use of knowledge, creativity, and technology was more advanced than what we have at the present time on Earth, and no other civilization has accomplished what the Atlantians achieved in science, art, music, and technology.

Unfortunately, most of the Atlantians had become focused on keeping their bodies going and had forgotten their source and who they really were. They knew how to move energy, suspend matter, and transport themselves across distances. They also played with mating the human form with animal forms. The results were not good and very sad. Atlantians also experimented with energy similar to nuclear power, but because of their great misuse, that energy is not available to the planet Earth now. Fortunately, the Earth was not very populated when they created an explosion that destroyed Atlantis and killed most of its people. Some Atlantians survived, as did the Lemurians, but there were many cataclysmic events that followed the initial explosion, which sent more souls Home.

I've already said that all energy is good. When good energy is used to violate the freewill and good energy of another, this is misuse. When the Atlantians caused their island to explode, every soul watching at Home said, "Now, wait. Since we are all one, with the same rights, each soul has a right to its own expression and perfection." So the misuse of energy had to be corrected to right use. This is the point in time when you, I, and everyone else in the All created debt. We decided that it was necessary to repay the energy that had been misused in order to regain balance. Over time, debt has been given many names by different religions. Christians refer to it as sin. Hindus call it "Papa" or "Moha." In Judaism, they call it "het" or "pesha." In Islam, there are over ninety words for offenses against others. In Buddhism, the word Karma is used. Regardless of the name you give it, any misuse you have created, you must "uncreate," fix, correct, redo, relive—just as long as you make it right.

Most Atlantians, in the destruction of their Earth place, returned to the All to think things over. They were welcomed Home by their fellow souls and thoughts began flying around as to why and how this creative adventure, which had been so good, had gone so wrong. They also discussed what they were going to do about all the misuse of energy, for it had to be re-balanced for everyone.

Well, a big think tank met and every light put in its "two-cents worth" of ideas. There was no right or wrong. It was just an exchange of ideas and opinions. Well, wait until I remind you of what we all decided to do next with our creative energy! We decided to back up—back way up—and start again. Everyone liked the body form, and agreed that it was a good start, but the use of the thinking mind was out of control. Like a kid with a new toy, we got a bit excited with the possibilities of what the mind could do and got carried away while playing with it. Of course, we then forgot about being spirit first and got sidetracked with our physical abilities, intellect, material things, and power so that we forgot everything else. Forgetting our source of energy and the All got us into trouble, as we created something we didn't want or couldn't handle and made a mess. Someone, somewhere, at some time, always has to clean up the mess, which is one of the "always." It is also where we got such common phrases as, "You reap what you sow," "What goes around, comes around," and "He'll get it one of these days."

So, those first brave souls who experimented first, because they could and because they had the freewill to do so, recorded every event of Lemuria and Atlantis—the good and the bad, the pretty and the ugly. Thus the record keeping began as a sort of universal accounting firm.

At this point, the records were set aside and everyone in the All agreed to back up and start over. Souls volunteered to rebuild a new and different body type, put their energy in it, and began the days of the Caveman! "What?" you say? Yes, yes, yes. Shocking, isn't it? But it's true. I'll stake my wings on it, and I love to fly.

You didn't rebuild life on Earth all at once after Atlantis and Lemuria. Instead, it was decided that things would be rebuilt upon a new, improved foundation to support all that was to come. But this time, it was going to be done very slowly.

Think about it; it makes sense. For example, if your house burns down and all your stuff is destroyed, you'd want to rebuild it better than before. During this re-creation of your house, you may improve it by adding a southern porch to enjoy the afternoon light, put in new windows, or add a guestroom. What has been destroyed by wind, fire, mud, or a cracking Earth is replaced quickly with ideas of, "I will begin again; I'll rebuild." You already have the spot, which is still okay. The foundation and plumbing are there. You also have help: insurance, friends, community and, of course, your own strong back and ideas.

In recent years, we've seen thousands lose their homes to floods, earthquakes, and other disasters, not to mention the disasters of man forgetting he is the same as his fellow man. Look at Kosovo. People have been forced to leave their homes, their country, and even their bodies—now that's big karma! The pain and devastation has been great; yet, in the deep layers of loss lies the thought of beginning again. Beginning again by burying the bodies, healing the injured, cleaning up the rubble, and going home again. How brave they are, how incredible, and how eternal the energy is to keep creating. You have done it more times than you can imagine. It's what and who you are.

Not all your fellow men have the same resources to begin again, but they do have help like the Red Cross, government assistance, and other giving individuals who come forth with aid; souls who have not forgotten that we are one.

Since you have the right to your own choices, you certainly wouldn't say to another, "Just make me a house to put my stuff in, and call me when it's ready." Oh no. You want an active role in creating this new place. How it will look, the materials it'll be made of, if it will be on a single floor or tri-level, a condo or a duplex, an apartment, cottage, or a mansion. It's your home and yours to design.

No matter how fantastic your designs, they all begin with a thought and your imagining of the end result. With rebuilding your house, you'll take your blueprints to the builder; however, the house won't go up overnight.

Just as one begins with a simple frame for a house, this time in creation, you began with a simple body form. You decided that souls in these bodies would first learn to use the supplies on the planet to survive, which would give them a better appreciation for water, plants, and animals. Now think of what you know of the caveman's life. It was based upon survival, wasn't it? The major concerns were eating, sleeping, and having sex or procreating. When a light chose to experience this life form, they did it to step back from the marvels of the Atlantian experience by evolving slowly to correct the previous misuse.

Over a long period of time, a primitive body type evolved. These cave people had no memory of purpose or of who they were first, because they were busy concentrating on the task at hand. To recall all that had come before would be too distracting and they would not have been able to focus on the moment in which they chose to live and learn. Those of you reading this now do not remember every moment and day of this life you are experiencing, and this is by choice. Again, your computer brain can only hold so much information. You designed it this way. All your memories can be tapped when you return Home as spirit.

Before computers or technology, the elders, libraries, and museums kept the records. Civilizations repeated stories to preserve an oral history. Then, the events were written down. Imagine that your grandmother saved every newspaper since she was seven years old and kept them in a stack in order. You want to find out when man first flew. She lived during that time, but wasn't aware of the event because she wasn't close to it or didn't hear about it. However, you know that it happened and want to know more. So, you and Grandma go through the stacks of newspapers to locate the story and get the details. It then becomes a part of your knowledge. You won't remember every word and detail of the story after a week's time, and you'll remember even less in a month. How much you need this information and how important it is to you determines how much you will remember.

26

As cavemen, we began again and did so with a plan to build a stronger foundation and to correct past misuses of energy. Picture the cave couple: there is not a lot to think about on a garden planet but that plants, when eaten, keep the body alive. Water washes it down and the rain, cold, and extreme heat hurt. They learned to get away from what was causing them pain by moving into caves or whatever was naturally available, which was a new thought. There was much experimenting going on, but making the physical body function was the first priority.

There was not a lot of thought and what thoughts existed were simple ones, like being close to one another keeps us warmer. Two pair of hands is better than one to pick food or catch animals to eat. The urge to be *really* close, in time, makes a cave baby, who will slowly grow and help out with daily life.

The physical life span was short for the caveman. After all, the body took a beating every day just awakening to eat and stay alive. Things were hard, and some of the big, ugly animals we had created wanted to eat us. But it was a good life because in the learning, misuse was being erased line by line by the record keepers. It was agreed upon by the All that this would be the way to go, step-by-step. Everyone was watching, learning, and thinking about when they'd jump in to do their share.

REMEMBER . . .

- Keep an open mind, be flexible in your thinking, and make room for new ideas.
- Who: The All/God.
- What: Creative Energy.
- When: A long, long time ago.
- Where: Heaven—Home.
- Why: Because you can, do, and will.

- How: Through your choices.
- We all made a place to go: Earth.
- We designed forms for our energy and understood who we were.
- We established outposts: Atlantis and Lemuria.
- We became caught up in the physical form and forgot about the Home energy source.
- We acted irresponsibly with the creation of energy, thoughts, and actions, and destroyed Atlantis.
- All the lights at Home rethought the Earth experience and recognized the power to play with energy.
- We came to a profound realization that misuse of energy makes more misuse, creating debt.
- The All reminded: "If you are going to create, you had better be responsible for your creations." Precious time must be spent to fix the screw-ups and clean up the mess.
- The All decided to begin again by recreating a new, slower plan. This new experience would be remembered and be a great lesson for All.
- The new experience begins; the caveman emerges.

Chapter 5

Early Physical Forms

There wasn't just one set of bodies designed by us to begin again. After all, we had made a really big planet full of terrific hills, dales, waters, and plants. Some couples spread out. We made those dinosaurs, too, which turned out to not be such a great and useful design. You know how groups are. There are always a few who get very carried away in creating. As it turns out, the dinosaurs were more destructive to the growth of the animal man. So, we voted and decided that it was time for them to head Home, and to choose another form in which to express themselves.

The dinosaurs were pretty magnificent, but not a good blend with what we were trying to accomplish at that time. So, when we see them in museums or movies, we glory in the memory of our sister souls who, at one time, said, "I have an idea!" This brings me to our brothers in rare form who, still to this day, walk the planet Earth, and who we call "The Abominable Snowman" or "Big Foot."

Remember, not all souls decided to experience energy on the planet Earth at the same time; therefore, not all souls are in the same form you are in, as you read this book. When an energy light decides to create a form for the first time, it does not just pop into that form, but rather starts off small and slowly evolves from there. At one point, some of you were Atlantians and cavemen and after you finished with those life forms, you went Home, reevaluated the next step, and made another form to try out. Sometimes, you would try the male experience and other times, the female experience, depending on what you wanted to learn. And, oh yes, the light of "you" goes farther back—from a spark of light to matter. Yes, first there was light. Always has been and always will be. We put the light in matter we created.

The "Abominable Snowman" or "Big Foot" life form does exist because there is yet a need for some souls to experience this physical expression. This body form lives in very small groups in remote areas and has a very rough life, much like the caveman's existence, but it is evolving. This race group continues to exist since they have a great love for one another. Souls from this race die, go Home, and remember who they are, and then choose to return to the same group because there are young ones who need teaching. This group and other remote tribes are crossover races that lie midway between the animal and plant kingdom and the human kingdom. Their goal is to develop their mental abilities, and as long as there is a need for this, they will exist. There are undiscovered tribes living in survival mode, and it is important that we understand that this is where these fellow souls are in their growth and that they should not be disturbed. The reason you should not disturb them is simple: just as you wouldn't want a Mars expression of energy coming to Earth to mess with your choice of life form, they don't want a human expression interfering with their choice of life form. It is the right, remember, of our fellow light beings to be whom and what they are, when and where, just as it is your right.

What you may find hard to understand, or can't seem to imagine, can be softened by acceptance. Stop, think, and remember: we are all one and the same; we're just using and expressing our energy differently. Now, isn't this comforting? So, don't get upset, the truth is simple. The object of showing you the history of our energy is that, first and foremost, you recognize in your fellow man—each and every one, everywhere, every time—that you are the same. You are just "doing it" differently by your choices!

All around you are souls who have experienced many different times on this Earth-school. Likewise, there are others who haven't been to "school" as often. Sometimes you hear one referred to as an "old soul" and another as a "new soul." Well, the truth is that we are all the same age! It's just that some may not have chosen to experience as much as others. When you use these terms, it is easier to say "old and young" because when a very experienced soul, for example, meets a far less experienced soul, he or she could be described as an ancient soul and the other, a baby soul. So, be sweet and kind. Remember that no matter where you are now, you were once where they are now. Be a real, cool soul; be patient, be a teacher, and applaud the efforts of those less experienced, just as more experienced souls marvel in all of your efforts

Some souls have chosen not to visit the Earth and have not put their energy into any physical form at all, as is their right. But they are still a part of us, and have chosen to stay Home. Some keep the records, watch us, send us more energy when we ask, and observe our progress with energy use and correcting our misuses. We often call these souls angels and guides.

Our stories, literature, and movies are full of images and references to these souls as a part of us, because you remember them and share this memory. They are the energy of help, love, and constancy. Angels welcome you Home, read the records, and teach and protect you.

Do you see why there are no secrets? Do you see that you are never alone? Every drop in that ocean of energy is vital to the All of energy. We all want the best experience for one another. How could we not, when we are the same? What hurts one, hurts another. What helps one, helps another. The energy of the All is a constant, ever-flowing exchange of energy that goes on and on. When you try to block it, stop it, or abuse it, the energy gets knotted and tangled until you take the time to fix it. Just like the kink in a garden hose, you have to go straighten it out so that the water will flow. Or like a dam in a creek, you're not going to get the water until you go break up the dam.

You helped create galaxies, planets, and star systems. Much work, thought, and creation went into building different body forms on many planets, including Earth. It was really fun tinkering around with a form we liked to put our energy into to use to experience life on Earth.

First, there were shadowy figures we used to explore the Earth in. Then, there were clusters of explorers and tribes here and there on Earth. After all, no one knew how the bodies would work, or what they would need to handle the physical properties of the Earth, like the weather and gravity. The souls were interested in how things worked in the physical world since it was so different from Heaven.

There are unlimited ideas in creation. It took millions of years to fine-tune the physical body form. Today, it is a very sophisticated life form, a wonderful miracle of engineering. Once we got the basic body down, there had to be some order. With order, came civilization, which is where Lemuria and Atlantis came into play.

You already know what happened to the Atlantians. Because of their fascination with their own intellect and technological advances, they forgot their link to Home, which ultimately led to their destruction. However, not everyone died in the destruction of Atlantis. Some survived, but not enough to continue their civilization. Descendants of Atlantis and Lemuria became ancestors to some Native American, Central American, and South American peoples. The soul energies that returned Home rethought, reviewed, and later used their knowledge of art, science, and technology in Roman and Greek civilizations.

The adventurous souls who decided they would "go first" into primitive bodies, did so in different areas on the Earth. They helped create fertile land and river valleys in India, China, Iraq, and Africa. Here, they began to relearn use of energy in body form. Shortly after entering into the physical body, man made time. You wanted and needed things in order; however, it is important to know that Earth time is not Heaven's time. These first days were not measured, but were watched carefully by all of us. It took eons for this new animal, man, to activate his new tool, the brain, and to think of how to survive in the body form.

Modern man has measured time in two blocks: BC and AD. BC refers to Before Christ, and AD, which is Latin for Anno Domini, means "in the year of the Lord." We will get into the great soul and teacher, Jesus Christ, later. For now, picture these blocks of time:

WBC (Way Before
Christ) —Planet Earth created
—Energy souls to Lemuria, Atlantis,
and other tribes

BC (40,000 years ago) —Caveman experience
—Neanderthal Man, Cro-Magnon
Man
—Time to evolve the physical and
mental

AD—Year 1—Year 30 —Jesus Christ leaves body
—Year 1000
—Year 1900
—Year 2000 NOW

Through this time, you have been involved in choices to create all that exists around you this very day. You and your fellow souls have chosen many Earth-school experiences to enjoy the learning and to correct the misuses. Each time you put your energy in a life form, you took with you all of your past experience and the energy of good things you accomplished, which Buddhists call dharma. You are also mindful of misuses of your energy—karma. Another name given this misuse is sin. These are words that awaken our thinking and that remind us that we must fix our misdoing.

You love yourself and are a part of the All. So, being an all-loving soul to yourself and others, you give yourself and fellow energies in the All every opportunity to grow and to fix mistakes. And we all decided to do this together repeatedly until we get things right.

You realized early on that it would be tough going it alone on the Earth-school, so like souls, with like ideas, came along to help. The more, the merrier, and sometimes the hairier! This is because it is easy to get caught up in all the stuff you created and to forget who you are. Oftentimes, misuse happens because you forget that your mom, boss, neighbor, child, or friend is a part of you. They are just like you, making different choices and experiencing life on Earth in different ways.

There is always a bigger picture and you had a thought in this, too. Just as there are blocks of time measured on the Earth of man's evolution, so there are also blocks of time in a bigger or higher framework that developed very slowly in the evolution of man's growth on the Earth. This framework is a natural flow of energy and awareness

There was a flow that this early life form experienced—a process that we continue to follow:

- Freewill—to choose the caveman body experience
- Intellect—developed very slowly, using the material

world to make things happen, thus you created the
wheel, fire, etc.

- Concrete Knowledge—"Wow, the wheel makes moving
  things easier! Fire keeps me warm. I'll do it again.
  What doesn't work, I will try another way."
- Harmony through Conflict—"My cave neighbor got a
  deer. I'm hungry. I will hit him if he won't give it to
  me. I will have a full stomach even if I have to kill
  him."
- Love, Wisdom—"Uh-oh! That hurt my cave neighbor
  when I hit him." Recognition of yourself in another.
  "He also needs food to be comfortable and in
  harmony. This knowledge tells me to be kind."
- Order—"Okay, I feel better now. We can share the food.
  We will hunt the food together and make rules. Our
  energies will work together. I understand."
- Devotion—"For our common good, we will help each
  other with the fire and food. If he does well, I do
  well. This works. We are all learning the same thing
  and are all devoted to the same idea, cause and
  purpose. This is ideal."

And today isn't much different, for example:

- Freewill—"That guy/gal attracts me. I think I'll ask
  him/her out."
- Intellect—Speaking the words, "Would you like to go
  out to eat with me? I will pick you up and we'll have
  a nice evening."
- Concrete Knowledge—"Wow! He or She said yes! He or
  She likes me too. We have a lot in common and I'd
  like to know more about his or her interests."
- Harmony through Conflict—"We have been dating for
  two months now and I do not like golf. Should I

stand her up? Refuse to play? OR maybe I can make it clear to her that I don't enjoy golf." So you talk and resolve the conflict and decide on things of harmony to do together.

- Love, Wisdom—"With each day we spend together, I learn wisdom, I love her or him more. All I think about gives me good thoughts."
- Order—"This relationship gives me balance. I am comfortable here."
- Devotion—"I want to commit myself to this person. We have the same goal."

Another example could be in connection to a job situation:

- Freewill—"I'll go to work at Tom's Gadgets Co."
- Intellect—"I know how to improve the blue gadget."
- Concrete Knowledge—"I'll test it first to make sure before I tell everyone."
- Harmony through Conflict—"Al doesn't think it will work. Sam thinks it will cost too much. Molly thinks it's ugly. I'll redesign, figure the costs, and show how it works well. Everyone agrees to try it."
- Love, Wisdom—"I took into consideration new ideas and suggestions. Now my blue gadget is better than ever."
- Order—"Let's get all the materials together to make it, produce it, and sell it."
- Devotion—"The blue gadget was a good idea. It makes people's lives easier. We will keep producing it for everyone."

Getting back to the caveman. In the time between hunting animals to eat, living in a cave, finding out that heat and friction make fire, that too hot and too cold hurts, that a wheel lifts burdens, and that really big animals are dangerous, the human body evolved both physically and mentally, as you created new thoughts and stuff all around you. One thought led to one thing after another. The learning time was very long, but that was by design to make it stick. As you found out the hard way: negative energy is quick to create and hard to change. Positive energy is slower, but holds firm once done. This was the slow route. While creating anew, you were fixing the past mistakes as you went along. All this time, making right the wrongs, paying back karma and debt, or experiencing a wrong doing you inflicted on another or yourself, you continued to learn and grow.

REMEMBER . . .

- You helped create all that is.
- Each soul grows at its pace.
- Allow everyone to experience as they choose.
- All souls are the same age.
- Baby souls vs. old souls amount to different degrees of experience.
- The Atlantians and Lemurians were early explorers of energy choices.
- Physical, mental, emotional, and spiritual evolvement happens over eons of time.
- Misuse of energy is karma. Do it over again and fix it.
- There is always a bigger picture.
- Energy flows through growth steps.

Chapter 6

Teachers—Those Who Show the Way

At certain points in history, an evolved fellow soul would take all his accumulated experience and come to the Earth-school to share it and teach others. The teachers presented a new way of thinking to help souls remember who they are. They spoke to the people of the time, as they could understand, presenting universal laws and truths.

The following teachers are presented in the order in which they lived. Since I, your Angel, was blessed with more information on Jesus, an additional section on him will follow the descriptions of the great teaching souls who lived before and after him.

Moses

Moses was a leader and prophet born in Israel about 1200 years before Jesus. As a baby, he was hidden in a basket on a river to save him from the Pharaoh who had ordered all Jewish baby boys to be killed. The Pharaoh's daughter found Moses and adopted him. He grew up in the royal household. He later killed an Egyptian who was beating a Jew. He left the town, met a gal, and married. While shepherding, he came across a burning bush where he encountered God. God told Moses to free the Jews from Egypt.

Ten plagues struck Egypt. The Pharaoh had had enough and allowed Moses to lead the Jews across the Red Sea. Moses was not only the leader of the Jews but also a political leader, lawmaker, and prophet. On Mount Sinai, he received God's teachings of the Torah and the Ten Commandments.

Buddha

Time marched on, and in 563 BC, in another part of the world, a prince was born in Nepal, India. He lived in luxury until he was 29 years old, and had a wife and son. The Prince's name was Siddhartha Gautama. One day, he saw a man who was old, another who was sick, and one who was dead. He began to question whether life was an unending cycle of aging, sickness, and death. To find out, he put on beggar's clothes and began to travel. He did not find teachers to help him, so he sat down to be quiet, to think, and to become enlightened, which is what the term "Buddha" means: "enlightened one."

In time, Siddhartha was awakened to the truth, as every soul has this ability. He had disciples. He was a physician who diagnosed ailments and pointed out paths to recovery. He also pointed out long cycles of time in which man moves, controlled by Karma, as a cause, moving toward freedom and salvation. One finds an end to suffering if he or she seeks something higher and eternal. He taught that no soul could be separate from the eternal energy. When one learns steps to truth, one should share them, teaching others.

Over time, Buddhism expanded to Tibet, China, Korea, Japan, Burma, and Thailand, with some differences in inter-pretation. The messages were "we live in suffering but it doesn't last" and that "reward and retribution is an ironclad law and *all* beings achieve salvation." The thought that all beings, no matter how depraved, could achieve salvation was a new thought in those days. Also, that there existed a "God" who would comfort in times of sorrow, give compassion and mercy during unfortunate times, and give hope and relief in the future from burdens of mundane life.

Devotion and meditation is a practice of Buddhist students. As Christianity has many interpretations, so, too, does Buddhism. People take what they can use now and apply it to their lives to understand why they live and how to better do so.

Confucius

In 551 BC, another teacher came to spread new thoughts on life and how to live it. K'ung Ch'iu, known as Confucius, was born near Shantung, China. Some people say that he was of humble birth, while others have said that he was born to a royal family; either way, he was a teacher of his day, looking for answers and sharing his findings. This was a time when only aristocrats had access to a formal education. They kept their knowledge, for it gave them power over others. Confucius wrote about morals, goodness, control of emotions, and the struggle of man to be his best. He brought forth the idea of men striving together to improve society. He sought kindness from those who had and knew more, and helped those less fortunate. His writings continue to be a moral and intellectual influence in Chinese society. The Confucian work ethic and loyalty to family have been credited with contributing to the success of economic development in East Asian countries.

Jesus

Jesus was born in Bethlehem, Israel, to Jewish parents. At a young age, he preached publicly and drew the attention of scholars. As a young man, he traveled great distances, meeting men and women of all beliefs, and briefly studied with Buddhist teachers in Tibet. He was a healer and teacher, and addressed God as his father, which others interpreted to mean that he was the "son of God." To the Jewish society in which he lived, this was blasphemy.

Jesus simply taught everyone to love one another and to

forgive in order to love more. He was considered a prophet and lived a very human life. His lifetime was one of everyman's, yet he was on a spiritual mission to show fellow souls new ways to think and behave towards one another.

After his death by crucifixion, his disciples traveled to spread his words. Christianity is the resulting philosophy.

Mohammed

About 570 years after Jesus lived, Mohammed was born in Mecca, Arabia. He was a sheep and camel tender. He later married a wealthy widow. At about age forty, he had a vision that told him to proclaim the one true Allah (God). He had to leave the town because of his beliefs, but later returned to Mecca with his followers and captured the city. He forbade the worship of idols. Non-believers were never to enter the city again. These groups of Muslims are the only ones allowed there even to this day.

Mohammed wrote his beliefs in the Koran, the holy book of Islam. He said that they were God's words, not his own. He said he was the messenger. Mohammed's teachings spread to Africa and Asia and within a hundred years of Mohammed's death, had spread to the Atlantic and borders of China. Mohammed saw with absolute clarity, that if God is God, there could only be one God. There cannot be a God of the Christians and a God of the Jews. The whole of Islam is based on this observation. There is only one God and all creation is derived from him. Therefore, all humans should live in unity. The word Muslim means "those who enter into a condition of safety because of their commitment to God."

At one stage, Islam's grasp of creation led to a passionate commitment to knowledge, which led to their achievements in philosophy and science. Muslim life teaches attachment to God in love and worship. The Muslims believed that before

Mohammed's message from God, the other prophets, Moses, Jesus, Buddha, and Confucius, brought similar messages. However, they believed that over time, those messages became corrupted and misused.

REMEMBER . . .

- *Moses*: Obey the commandments and all will be well with you. If you don't, it won't.

- *Buddha*: No soul can be separate from God. God is loving.

- *Confucius*: Men strive together to improve society. Kindness from those who have and know more, to those who have less.

- *Jesus*: Love one another. Treat every living thing as perfect and a part of the All and you.

- *Mohammed*: There can only be one God. All humans should live in unity.

Chapter 7

Judaism

During and after Confucius and Buddha, civilizations were building in Egypt, Greece, Rome, Turkey, and Jerusalem. In Greece, a fellow named Pericles thought up democratic ideas as a way for people to govern themselves. In Italy, the rivalry of warring cities caused the shift of power to Rome, where the Romans came up with a central and united form of government, with good communications and a strong defense. Later, as Rome's northern neighbors began to overrun Italy, the power shifted to Constantinople, which is now Istanbul, Turkey. The Roman Empire had five provinces. Rome (Italy), Alexander (Egypt), Antioch (Egypt), Constantinople (Turkey), and Greece. The title "patriarchs" was assigned to the authorities over these territories.

The patriarchs and matriarchs of Jerusalem were Abraham and Sarah, Isaac and Rebekah, and Jacob and Rachel. These three couples are the ancestors of the Jewish people. The Jews share a family tree and their book of guidelines is the Torah. The Torah's bottom line is: "That which is hateful to you, do not do to your neighbor."

Judaism, in time, branched off into different groups of ideas, much as Buddhism had. There is now Orthodox, Reform, Conservative, Progressive, Reconstructionist, and Liberal Judaism. No matter what differing beliefs or guidelines are used to conduct their lives, the Jews all agree that they are inseparable from Israel. They are very separate from Christianity and Islam in any form. They were tribes of people and began to settle, unite, and conquer territory.

There were many, many rules and rituals every day to be a faithful Jew. But the Jewish faith of ethics and obedience were strong and growing when Jesus was born. All Jews, no matter their interpretation of their faith, believe that God would send a Messiah to unite them all and their land. This made the Romans very nervous. The Jews and Romans fought and Rome won the Holy Land of the Jews. The Jews' holy book, the Torah, is a language of love, a way of saying yes to God. (At this time in its beliefs, there was no reward of being with God after death.) The Jewish philosophers stressed faith and the quest for wisdom and truth. One is born to the Jewish faith. They do not recruit followers, but do allow converts.

And so now we have on our evolving timeline over years, three different ways of thinking. The man on Earth (who had forgotten) tries to figure out why he is on the Earth and what comes after. The thinking mind is well developed and there is great mastery in many regions on Earth of its materials.

Chapter 8

Jesus

There were different groups of beliefs on the Earth at the time that Jesus, the teacher, was born to a Jewish household with a father Joseph, who was a carpenter, a mother Mary, and younger brothers and sisters. Jesus had a deep understanding of the Torah, the teachings of the Jewish religion.

Before Jesus, Mary, and Joseph were in body form on Earth, they had a meeting and set up their life paths and missions. They decided what they would accomplish together and how they would help and support one another, just as you did with your family, and choosing your parents, circumstances, and situations from which to act upon, experience, and learn. Every soul, even Jesus, Mary, and Joseph's, are in a constant state of becoming and perfecting. These three souls had lived lifetimes before, just as you have. Their souls are just as much a part of you as every soul in your life.

At this time in man's growth, some new ideas needed to be presented to help all souls in body form to move forward in new thought. Jesus volunteered to help bring about these needed changes. He had the desire and strength of spirit to put himself in body form on Earth as a real baby, with a real family, real challenges, and problems of the day. He chose to bring to Earth, hold onto, and teach by example and word, the Christ Consciousness. The Christ Consciousness is a soul energy that has reached a time in soul growth of overall understanding of what it's all about! "Christ" is a title meaning, "anointed one." "Consciousness" means to know, or to have knowledge. Jesus ate, slept, breathed, and demonstrated the Christ Consciousness every day of his life on Earth. He met, reacted, replied, and treated every living being as perfect, a part of the All, and a part of Him. In any day and age, this is difficult, because a person can get bogged down in doubt, pain, grief, beauty, money, and all the personality games that are a part of the human body package.

Jesus, Mary, and Joseph discussed his mission in spirit form before they "took the plunge" to set it all in motion. Mary had her plans, too. She wanted to experience all aspects of a nurturing motherhood this lifetime. If all went according to their plan, she wanted to help support the mission of her son's life. In doing so, she also would serve quietly as a good example of a wife and mother. Joseph's life plan was to support and protect Mary, while she was pregnant with Jesus. With his quiet, happy, and hardworking personality, he would be a good provider, husband, citizen, and father. He would set a good example for generations to emulate. Joseph was a sturdy and loving man who knew how to trust his intuition. He had a good understanding of what he'd come to do. This understanding wasn't on a conscious level that he could discuss with people, but the decisions in this life "felt right." He was a man very attuned with the world he lived in.

So the three decided that Joseph would be born on Earth first, learn all he could, and become established. When he was about eleven years old, Mary would join an Earth family close by. Then, when she was fourteen, she would fulfill her agreement with the energy of the Christ Consciousness to become pregnant, through creative idea and thought to bring the body of Jesus without having sex with Joseph. Pretty neat use of energy! So, the "virgin birth" is true. In this time, most women were very protected by their families. It was a family or tribe's project to match men and women for marriage. Women were stoned to death for lesser offenses than being pregnant and not married.

This virgin birth caused Mary a lot of problems. Who knows what the town gossips said? However, Mary and Joseph were engaged and Joseph was a businessman, and commanded a quiet respect. In their hearts and minds, they both knew that the pregnancy was okay and right. They were about their mission. Their attitudes, characters, and personalities did not allow the circumstances of her pregnancy to be a huge problem.

At the time Jesus, Mary, and Joseph lived on Earth, people did not usually live to be very old. Health, sanitation, disease, and food supplies were not what they are now. Girls were considered women at thirteen and fourteen years of age, and began to marry and have children. Boys learned skills to barter at thirteen and fourteen. By the time a person was twenty-five, he or she was viewed as we would see a forty-year-old of today.

The middle-aged and good man Joseph was one of the well-established twenty-five-year olds of his day. He was considered an older bachelor and a good catch. Many families had their eye on him for their daughters. Joseph's tribe or community recognized him as a leader, a dependable person who was good at taking care of things. He had chosen not to marry because, in his heart, he knew the time was not right.

Joseph was busy building his mill business. He would cut trees, and would sometimes buy the wood needed to build furniture or other wanted items for sale or barter. He saved and though not wealthy, he was a man of prosperity.

Mary was fifteen when she and Joseph married. Joseph believed in working hard and following the laws to the letter. That is why there was no question in his mind when word came that he and Mary must make the trip from Nazareth to Bethlehem to register for the census, even though the baby

Mary was carrying might be born away from the family. They made the trip and on the way, Mary delivered the baby Jesus. It was not a remarkable birth or unusual in any way. Today, it is portrayed very dramatically, but in truth, the whole world as it was then, did not know that a "King" was born. There was no Internet or CNN to zap the news across the ethers, even if people would have believed it.

Mary and Joseph were a normal couple and loved one another. Jesus was the first of their six children. About a year or two after Jesus was born, Mary and Joseph had another son, Abraham, then in "stair steps," two more sons, Judeah, nick-named Jude, and Milos. So the "old" bachelor, who had waited until the time was right, started a family with Mary. It was what they both wanted and for what Joseph had been waiting.

Their children were of great joy to them. A dark-haired and dark-eyed sister, Sarah, joined the four sons a few years later. Then, after many years, Joseph and Mary, at age thirty-two, had a surprise baby—Anna. Jesus and his brothers had fun roughhousing and growing up together. Sarah was a gentle influence on Jesus' life and they were good friends.

Jesus was different physically from his parents and siblings. He not only didn't look like them, but he was unusual. When Jesus did something to embarrass them, they were all mortified, such as, when Jesus would make pronouncements while at the temple.

Joseph trained his sons in the milling and carpentry business. They enjoyed the creativity of working with wood. But Jesus would act differently and Joseph would get upset and think, "What has happened? What is wrong with him?" As a good father and a loving man, Joseph would try to understand his son. Throughout this, Mary and Joseph tried to mold the children into a family unit, but there was no doubt that Jesus was the odd one out, the black sheep, the outsider. It was most likely a dysfunctional family, but not the first!

Joseph was very disappointed when Jesus did not follow in his occupation. Abraham was a physically big man when he grew up and worked with Joseph, Jude, and Milos. Jesus and Abraham were the closest and best of friends, but Abraham worried about Jesus. He thought Jesus was a little crazy and would go to his mother and ask, "Do you think Jesus is okay?" Mary would tell Abraham that they had to let him follow God in his own way.

Abraham was a good soul, but was not interested in the teachings of Judaism and study. It was not his thing. Jesus was just their brother and he was doing his thing. They were not all that interested in his teachings. Jesus left home at a young age and traveled to Tibet and India. He worked in fields along the way for his food. He was very much a part of the physical world and worked in it. He had to experience and understand the world. He had to know what everyday life was really like for his fellow man. He had to know the troubles they faced in order to preach and teach. He got around to many places and knew a lot of people personally.

Jesus found it interesting that, in the Buddhist monasteries, they shut themselves off from the world. However, he gained much knowledge and understanding there. It was a time in his life to deepen spiritually. His life plan was to be out among people. A problem when he began preaching was that people would hear him and say, "How can this guy be a teacher? He worked in my fields. What does he know?"

Jesus walked and talked. During his life, he walked about 2,400 miles from Jerusalem to Northern India and then to Tibet. When you think of it, that's about the distance from New York to Los Angeles! The reason for going so far was that Jesus had heard of the Buddha's teachings and wanted to visit his birthplace, the Garden of Lumbini, near the foot of the Himalayas. He was talking and listening to people and thinking about other's beliefs.

While in this area, he became ill with a fever and was left by friends at a monastery of Buddhist monks. A sage told him he would have to heal himself and look for the perfection in his own true being. At this point, Jesus had not grasped the whole concept of healing himself. He was given teas and vegetation for the physical body, but this did not wholly heal him. At this point, he had a vision and saw another part of himself, a thought form, which led to his concept of three levels of energy within the body. What he was slowly coming to understand was the existence of the emotional with the mental and physical.

Now Jesus had been through many lifetimes and had evolved in his soul growth, but what he had to do was to draw back and take time to contemplate what he had learned and how it was fitting into his current mission. When he came to better understand his role and healed himself, he said good-bye to his first teacher, the Buddhist monk, and continued with his travels through India.

When Jesus returned to the area where his family lived, he would visit. All his siblings were married. Sarah had married at age fourteen and had only two children, which was unusual in this time. She was not in good health and had family responsibilities, so she did not follow Jesus. She did hear him preach though, as did Joseph shortly before his death.

As a widow, Mary lived in her children's households. Abraham and his wife wanted Mary with them most of the time because they knew people were talking about Jesus' ministry, and that the officials in the area didn't like it. Jesus had many followers, besides the apostles, with whom Mary was friendly.

The family lived outside of Jerusalem and Jesus was warned that people didn't like him. Of course, he knew this as he continued to fulfill his life purpose. They all had a family gathering and Jesus told his family that he thought his time was short. They all agreed with him! "Keep talking like you do, and someone is going to kill you!" Since he was their brother, they were all concerned with Jesus' criticism of the authorities; they knew that what he was saying was dangerous.

Abraham tried to turn Jesus from his purpose, and offered him a home with his family. They thought Jesus odd, but they were worried and afraid for him. Abraham offered to re-teach him carpentry and to help him establish a different life. He wanted to help his brother get away from the path he was on. No one in the family wanted to see their brother die, and told Jesus he didn't have to do this. This temptation to have a normal life was one of the temptations he wrestled with, but the Christ Consciousness was strong in him and he continued on.

When Jesus left for Jerusalem, the rest of the family stayed where they were. Sarah was grief stricken and very afraid for her brother. Mary accompanied the apostles, for she knew it was the beginning of the end for Jesus, and it was part of her mission to be there for her son throughout all of his ordeals.

Though she was his beloved mother and he was her special, dearest son, she was very distraught. From time to time, Mary had traveled with Jesus on his walks and had come to know the apostles well. She knew she was needed with the apostles at this time to help hold them together. It was a terrible time for all of them and there was a chance that if their human weaknesses took hold through their fear, it might affect Jesus' mission.

Remember, these were real people with friends, in-laws, neighbors, fears, worries, health issues, job problems, kids going wild, all the while surrounded by a political system that punished opposition quickly in horrible, gross ways. Through the eyes to the soul, you are perfect. Jesus and the apostles were human, like you, but they learned and taught that if you express spirituality through physical expression and your personality, all will be well.

Jesus never spoke ill of his fellow men behind their back. He never tried to be what he wasn't. He was a big, jolly, happy man who loved children and the life force energy. He was a simple man and had a message that appealed to people of this time on Earth. He was a deep thinker and knew that love is the most powerful energy. He loved himself, the light of his soul, and the challenge of this mission. He gave his energy freely to all who wanted it and was totally committed to his life plan, even when he didn't understand it completely. His brothers considered him a wanderer, a "hippie." He lived his life simply, step-by-step, day-by-day, and tried to lift up each life he met with some of his energy.

No one has ever forgotten him. We measure our years by him, before his life on Earth, and after. He left each person he touched with a positive energy. He had a personality, got angry, and had a temper. He handled his anger alone. He is to be seen as a man and a teacher. He had to keep going or he knew the energy he brought would be for nothing. His steps took him to the day of sacrifice, so you would remember and recall what he had taught.

Only those who could "hear" Jesus' teachings followed him. There was only word of mouth at that time, so no one heard the same thing the same way. All those who heard Jesus' teachings took away ideas that they could understand and use, which is also true for the followers of Confucius and Buddha. When the student is ready, the teacher is provided. When the soul is ready to take the next step in growth, it searches out the answers—just as you are searching by reading this book and learning and remembering more. Then, the lessons must be applied to oneself and others in everyday life.

But let's get back to what Jesus was doing. So, here you have a Jewish community under Roman authority that has been trying to be good, while at the same time, trying to follow their beliefs. Now Jesus comes along after he's been out asking questions of his elders and searching out other ways of thinking, and he speaks of the kingdom of God, calling God "King" and "Father." Since he is calling God "Father," people begin to think that he feels that he is the Son of God. This is not what Jesus meant to have happen, though. He understood that God is All and that each of you, as a part of the All, is a child of God, a spark of the universal light. He then started using God's authority to be a healer and hung out with people who were generally considered undesirables by the society of the time. He preached forgiveness and served as an example of good-ness, which attracted and transformed the lives of others.

What Jesus wanted to do was simplify faith, to remove the confusion that many of the Jewish laws caused for individuals seeking answers for themselves. He summarized the Torah as being the love of God and the love of one's neighbor. However, he added that this love could be drawn from God to heal and forgive. This idea threatened the decision-makers, the rabbis, of this time, because it implied a direct relationship between God and humans through one's own self. This was the offense that shook the leaders of Jerusalem, as it threatened their authority. They questioned whether his teachings were from God or from men.

The laws of the day were such that if you insisted on your own opinion against the majority, you would be brought before a judge and executed if you did not reject those opinions. It was believed that two interpretations of the Torah would destroy Israel. The high priests questioned Jesus, who was silent, letting all he had spoken stand. Jesus knew he was directed by God, the All energy, and that his life, examples, and lessons were necessary to help his fellow souls think in a new way and to move forward in their soul growth.

Though the Jews competed with the Romans as they lived together, Jesus' ideas threatened both groups. He threatened the Jews' religion and the Romans' control of the area. To safeguard their religious authority, the Jews turned Jesus over to the Romans for punishment, where he faced crucifixion, the cruel and humiliating punishment reserved for dangerous outlaws.

Pontius Pilate was the Roman Governor in Jerusalem when Jesus lived. He didn't want to have anything to do with the death of Jesus because he recognized something in Jesus' energy. As a result of this, Pontius Pilate relinquished his responsibility for making the decision to kill Jesus. However, his own conscience had already been touched and his thoughts tossed from mental to emotional, and emotional to mental, over and over out of guilt, which nearly drove him mad. Since he couldn't take his thoughts higher and get out of the vicious cycle he was in, Pontius Pilate passed from the world shortly after Jesus' death. He did not know that he could ask for help from his higher self, that all he had to do was to think: "Help me to find a new idea to get past this repeating cycle I am in."

Over two thousand years ago, Jesus died on a cross, and he died knowing his source and knowing that he is eternal. He used his body as a vehicle to teach his fellow souls how to evolve in their growth. He taught love and tolerance and forgiveness for everyone by everyone. The energy of his example has not been forgotten, but has been repeated through all the years since his death. As "Christ" means anointed one, Jesus was showing everyone he met that each of us is a "Christ," that each soul is special and part of the All.

Over the hundreds of years since Jesus walked the Earth, there have been many divisions in how to interpret his teachings, but the bottom line has always been: "Love God and your neighbors."

Man likes to put his personality and trust in his opinions. So the New Testament, the Christians' book of guidelines, was interpreted and reinterpreted. It was originally written in Greek, the language of scholars in Jesus' day, and not in English, thus how it was translated has affected how individuals read or hear it. It also depends on where the individual is in his or her soul growth to accept and use Jesus' teachings, or any other teacher on Earth for that matter. Your neighbor, spouse, child, and friends could be your teachers.

REMEMBER . . .

- Jesus, Mary, and Joseph planned their lifetime mission before coming to Earth.
- New ideas needed to be presented.
- Jesus brought the Christ Consciousness to Earth and taught people by word and example.
- Jesus was close to his family but always different.
- He spoke to elders and traveled to understand the world.
- Jesus taught love and forgiveness.
- His teachings and examples are the basis for Christianity.

Chapter 9

Old and New Ideas

This book that you hold in your hand is another learning tool. It is not meant to be a scholastic or deep, theological text, but rather a simple collection of words that can help you as you search for understanding at this point in your life. Knowledge is wonderful if you use it. If you don't, it just sits there.

At some point in time, religions began to teach the idea of hell and of each man having only one life. The idea was that if you do wrong, there is no chance to make it right, which results in going to a place called hell and suffering forever for your mistakes. In addition, if you only live one lifetime, that's all you've got, so you'd better make the most of it and follow the straight, narrow, and prayerful path.

These concepts were taught to help people do better, but also to control them. Religions that say "believe in my way—I am your leader" can be wonderful avenues to goodness and right living. They remind us of what we truly are and that the energy of loving one another is of the utmost importance. Some groups can get off track, however, and in the name of religion, judge others, forgetting that we are all one and the same. There have been religious leaders, and groups, who have done horrible things to their fellow man in the name of God and religion.

How can there be a hell? How could a loving God or All energy punish you? The truth is that you each create your own hell through misdeeds and misuse of your energy choices. An individual's hell is to fix those misdeeds by becoming the one who is the receiver of misuse, to experience the same pain, worry, or conflict that was inflicted upon another. Thus the sayings: "What goes around, comes around," "She'll get what's coming to her someday," and "You reap what you sow." It is the balance, righting, and correction of misdeeds and energy misspent. Remember, the Akashic records are kept by our fellow souls to help us keep the balance. If someone has hurt you deeply, they will and must, somewhere in time, experience the same to correct their misuse of good energy. However, that time can be thousands of years from now. Man's soul is eternal, and he exercises freewill. The divine law says one must be responsible for his or her creative energy choices. If you cheat, steal, kill, lie, damage, or hurt another fellow soul, the only way you can right the situation is to experience that same pain in order to understand and right your misuse.

How are you going to do this by coming into a physical body one time, dying, and then going Home to the All? Wouldn't a truly loving Father (the All) give its beloved souls every chance to be the best they can be? Of course. So, when your Earth-school life ends, you are your own judge of how you used your energy in your own lifetime. You decide how you are going to fix your mistakes. You choose another life and circumstances to be "born" into that will give you opportunities to perfect your soul's energy.

Each time you enter a new school lifetime of learning, you know you are taking a risk again. You have the opportunity to erase the wrongs, but you also have the opportunity to create new mistakes. Living here on the Earth-school is a tricky business. The goal is to undo the misuses and build a bank of good deeds so that you can go home and stay there in harmony with the All energy. You can experience any creation or galaxy you desire. It is all yours.

Buddha and Jesus did this. There was no reason for them

to return. Like you, they had lived many times before. Some souls you know from the Bible, such as the belligerent Pontius Pilate, Judas, and the thief on the cross, needed to return again and again to make right their harmful choices. Pontius Pilate and Judas are at Home for good now. That thief is still working on it. The other thief who hung with Jesus that day, and chose to accept who Jesus was, did indeed unite with Jesus at Home by the day's end. His soul growth leaped as he recognized the All energy in Jesus, God, himself, and all men. This was all his soul needed to complete his Earth-school experiences. Some are fast learners and some are slow. You have every right to the time you need to learn and grow.

This is what pure, unconditional love is—recognizing the absolute best in everyone and where they are in their soul growth, and always giving them their right to make choices. This is very hard to do in the material world you have created. There are so many distractions and temptations to move you away from whom and what you are, and your mission. There are many paths to travel and many choices to make. However, deep down in that quiet place just beyond your heartbeat, you know that you are very special, worthy, loving, and whole. When the layers of flesh, personality, and earthly desires are pulled away, who are you? You know! The best of you is so strong, pure, good, giving, and powerful, that you can do anything. The trick is to truly recognize this in yourself and everyone else.

People traveled the planet learning other people's ways of thinking and living. The Chinese dynasties developed. The civilizations in Russia and England advanced. Often, they clashed over "I will make you believe and live the same way I do." Man was forgetting the right of choice, as harmony was struggling to come through conflict.

Judaism permitted the Jews to be moneylenders and the

Christian faith did not. That made the Jews unpopular. The Christians got it in their heads that the Jews were directly responsible for killing Jesus so persecuting the Jews became a commendable religious act and still takes place to this day. The first country to expel Jews was England. The thought during the Crusades was, "Let's all go trekking across the lands together and get rid of, or convert, these nonbelievers, or those who don't think like us." Pope Urban II inspired people to go to where Jesus lived and walked (Palestine) and to throw out the Muslims.

Much was thought, done, and created in the name of religions. Temples, mosques, and cathedrals were built to serve man in worship. Beautiful structures and great intentions were always visible in tribes of man looking beyond himself for more.

By now, man had conquered the use of his physical body. Some went way beyond a cave for comfort, to great palaces. The thinking mind had leapfrogged ahead from thoughts of survival to that of great space, astronomy, and philosophy. The human condition is to want to share what one knows, whether it is a new invention, knowledge, or gossip. Word of mouth was the teacher from generation through generation. The thinking mind developed the written pictures, then words, to record what was discovered and learned by a generation.

You have to remember that in different locations on the Earth, different groups and civilizations were living and developing their ways of handling their learning experiences on Earth. These group ways of thinking and doing things are often called group consciousness or race consciousness. You can all relate to this in your own family. Grandparents have the mindset of their days—behavior, manners, rules, and sayings. Then, your parents have their set of guidelines, which may differ somewhat from yours. Your children's ideas will be different. Ideas are repeated or deleted. What is repeated is not always good, such as bad language or judgments of others. What is repeated becomes the foundation of your family group's way of thinking and behaving.

For example, today, we would agree that slavery is wrong. Of course it is, as it deprives people of their freewill to make choices. In the United States, the people in the 1860s went through harmony, then conflict, to change how man treated his fellow man. They killed one another—one side, to change misuse, another, to keep it. But those Southern souls had a mind set and group consciousness about slavery. Many places in this century still do. One doesn't have to have dark skin to be a slave. The Jews were slaves to the Egyptians. Perhaps these Egyptians came into African bodies to be enslaved later in time to experience this condition, repay their misuse, and to know firsthand what it was like.

A hundred and fifty years after the U.S. Civil War, there are still people that hold onto this mindset, because they have heard repeated negative remarks about African Americans. And this is not only in the South. If groups don't move ahead in love, wisdom, and understanding, they repeat thinking and behavior until a lesson is learned. It doesn't change until someone thinks differently and shares and uses that knowledge.

You can be the one in your family to alter a negative pattern. Maybe being very critical of others is a family pattern. You can change it by not criticizing others and by being a good example. By speaking up and not approving of what others do, you demonstrate another way of thinking. Instead of being negative or nasty about another's differences, find the good and positive about them.

History shows that it takes hundreds of years, even thousands, for mankind to alter a thought in a new direction. This is always happening. It is happening now. One day beyond your years on Earth, mankind will evolve to really see himself in his fellow man and honor it. One day, all the races will be blended and one's ancestry, no matter what is, will be revered because man will know enough to say, "How interesting that you chose this body, this skin, this place, and this family, to repay any debts and grow spiritually."

Right now, you can't imagine it, but it will come to pass. It's like our thoughts are a gazillion-piece puzzle, and one day all the pieces will fit in place to make one big picture of the All. Every single energy soul light is included in it, to make it perfectly complete. Then we create again.

Where are you now in this scheme of life? Freewill got you here on a planet you created. There are souls on the Earth and souls in the All. Since souls live on Earth in many forms, why not in other places? Souls can actually take themselves to other galaxies and planets and live in different forms. There are no limitations to your use of creativity and choices. Remember that thoughts are real things.

In the world today, there are great strides being made by man that seem miraculous, from technological advances to space exploration. Yet, at the same time, on Earth, hidden in the deep jungles, there are souls who are just starting out that need a primitive experience based on everyday survival. These are young souls with intelligence who need room to grow and should not be disturbed. To interfere with their natural soul growth experience upsets the flow of their life plan.

Explorers and missionaries in the past, and even now, have invaded these people's expressions of life, creating confusion and problems. You would not ask or expect a baby to drive a car! They are not there yet. You would wait until the child grows and develops and is capable. Just as your soul growth took time, and as you began at the beginning, so are some of your fellow men. So the right thing to do is to rejoice in their choice and to accept where they are in learning.

The intellect developed and knowledge accumulated and was written down for the next soul's use. This knowledge often led to hierarchies of power, and using power to control and lead those less knowledgeable. There are always people at every level of development. The one who is the tallest, richest, thinnest, and most loved is not necessarily the one with a bank full of positive soul growth. This is just their own reflection of who they are in this lifetime. The person beside you, as you read this, or next door, or at work, could be the most glowing, shining soul in an ordinary life with average appearance, fulfilling his or her last Earth-school experience. The thing is, you don't know. Outwardly, this person's habits and personality may not show what you would expect of an old soul. As many souls as there are, there are as many choices and ways of expression. The common denominator is the energy of love, and people express love in many ways.

Souls on the Earth-school learn best through trial and error, action and reaction, harmony through conflict. Perhaps the soul was an alcoholic in its last lifetime and neglected the family, cheating them out of attention, love, and money. This time, he or she is the family member to realize the pain of this misuse and imbalance. The conflict is the imbalance and misuse. The righting of it creates harmony and knowledge. With knowledge and wisdom comes love and understanding. Once one realizes and understands that they have a problem and must fix it, there is order in thinking and doing. Ideally, this leads to service, teaching, and helping others—devotion. The recovering alcoholic may become a counselor to other alcoholics.

This is easy to "see" in an individual sense. But at the same time, all souls decided at Home that there would also be huge blocks of energy development for groups working together to live and learn through.

—The Cave Man	Freewill
—Early Civilizations	Intellect
—Philosophers, Prophets, Thinkers	Knowledge
—BC to AD through 1900s	Harmony through Conflict
—1990 to present	Love—Wisdom
—The Future	Order and Devotion to All

Man is still moving out of the harmony through conflict energy. Get out a history book and list all the wars, conflicts, and police actions. One group would war against another because they didn't think or believe the same things, or they would forcibly take something from another, and this happened repeatedly. There were winners and losers and afterwards, something changed. Most of mankind has learned that there are better ways to change things to get what they want. It took war after war—recording it, examining what went right or wrong, and seeing what was gained or lost. What hurts more: Being hit by a rock or an atom bomb?

Man's thinking is evolving to look both within and without. More people today ask, "What am I doing here?" "Who am I?" Wise governments are finding new ways to stop misuse without force, and teaching others to do the same. Of course, not every group thinks this way and is yet caught up in the conflict energy. People that have learned serve as examples and teachers. If you don't know history, you will repeat it. We are all repeating it until we get it right and change it. So very gradually, souls are thinking, feeling, and expressing love through their accumulated wisdom. It has been necessary to go through all these stages physically and in soul growth.

The baby doesn't run from his mother's womb. First, he lifts his head, then rolls over, scoots about, crawls, pulls himself up, stumbles about, takes a few steps, falls, balances, walks, skips, and then runs! The intellect also develops in stages. The baby hears sounds. Sounds become language. Language becomes babbling. Babbling becomes words. Words become sentences. The letters become written language. The written word expresses thought. The thinker reads the words to learn more.

Man has learned, in the last fifty years, how the mental, physical, and emotional aspects of man work together. Not long ago, if someone acted strangely, they were simply removed from society to a protected place. Gradually, it was learned that mental ideas could cause emotional pain and make the physical body sick. When all three are in balance, the body is whole and works properly.

An example of imbalance is when the mind begins to think, "I am so busy. I can't do it all." The emotions are expressed through tears, sleep, anger, and impatience. If not, the physical body can get sick because the negative, out-of-balance emotions have to go somewhere. The physical body is the foundation for holding the soul's energy on the Earth plane. Emotions are a pool of energy from which to draw, to put thoughts into actions and to help change things. There is a constant interchange between the mental and the emotional. "She loves me, she loves me not." You think it, feel it, and act it. Where the flow gets messed up is in how you choose to act on your thoughts with your emotional makeup. When the mind and body are at ease, it is functioning well. When it is not, it is in *dis*-ease.

Now, hold these thoughts a while and be reminded that whatever your circumstances in your life at this moment, you have created them through a series of thoughts and choices that began before you were in this physical form, and even choices in previous life experiences. This may be a hard thing to think about. Try again to open your mind and be flexible in your thinking. You may have to push aside some old thoughts to make room. But give it a try, as you are a remarkable soul oozing with loving energy and just trying to learn how to express it differently.

You created positive and negative to have balance. If there were no cold, you wouldn't recognize hot. If there were no bad, you wouldn't know good. Some souls, as is their right, choose to express negative energy. This is easier to do because the responsibility for its use is not taken, even though there are repercussions for misuse. It is more difficult to be mindful of one's responsibility of choices and not blame others. Be aware of your fellow man's rights. The essence of evil, the devil, Satan, does exist. This energy choice is negative, though those who use it this way are still a part of us. Because it is negative, it must feed off positive to keep going.

Picture a dark room as negative energy. You can't see in it. You need light, positive energy, in order to avoid tripping over the furniture. You can't add more dark to dark, you can only take away light. Here and there you get light from a candle or lamp to see your way clear. The room can get brighter and brighter with the more light you add.

Negative people busy themselves sapping up positive energy, light, from positive people to see their way a while longer and to keep being negative. They can take the energy out of your room (you), and put you in the dark (hurt, sadness, anger). When you allow them to do this, you have to work all the harder to restore yourself in balance.

Aunt Acidy comes to visit. She's a very unhappy woman. She doesn't like children. You are sixteen. She criticizes your hair, clothes, friends, weight, and manners. You were happy about yourself until she showed up. She makes you feel insecure, unpopular, ugly, fat, rude, and unstylish. Geech! So you may become teary, sad, and mean. Aunt Acidy is fine. She feels superior. She just sucked the light right out of you.

You have the right to think well of yourself. She doesn't have the right to tip your balance. To get it back, you can talk positively to yourself. Ignore her words, remind yourself of your assets, and pump yourself up to a good self-image. You have reacted mentally and emotionally. Then, being the heavenly All creature you are, you can take your Aunt and her words one step higher! You may think, "Poor Aunt, she's had it rough and is negative. Maybe if I love her more than others do, she will be kinder." This extra step is pulling forth the best from your energy source. When this is done, it is easier to recuperate from the mean treatment and harsh words. If you don't respond at all, you do not feed the negative energy. This is difficult to learn to do. Often, it takes a person many hurtful experiences to learn to reject negative energy from others, or how to block it and avoid being detoured from the path.

Remember that some souls have chosen not to be in a physical body form. They are all energy and thought. These helpers have had many names throughout history and in different beliefs. Angels, divas, fairies, guides, messengers. All are helpers who have chosen to serve their fellow souls. Some souls have finished up. That is, rounded out and perfected their soul by paying back past debts and experiencing different race consciousness groups and learning about the power of their energy—love. These souls chose to stay Home in the All. But this isn't the end. There is never an end. As long as one soul is thinking and creating, the energy keeps on going. Perhaps when you are all done with this planet, you may try out another life form creation in which you wish to express yourself.

Some souls at Home are exploring, learning, teaching, traveling, serving, sitting, or being. It is up to them. There is no rush. There is no time. There are groups of souls that welcome souls Home from Earth-school living. There are souls that pool their energies to send positive action thoughts to troubled places on Earth. There are souls that help those finished on the Earth to leave the body and come Home. Each soul on the Earth-school has a soul in Heaven to watch and deliver energy as asked for, and some, a group called the Lords of Karma, keep the records for you to review when you go Home to see how you did. There is a lot going on. Where is it you think you go when your body must sleep to re-energize and refresh? The essence of you, the higher, true you, floats Home to recharge and be enlightened if one is of this awareness. To sleep, pray, meditate, dream, visualize, or to rise up and out of the physical world is to reach for and check in with Home, to draw on one's source. When one completes an Earth-school life and goes Home, one doesn't need to return to Earth if it isn't one's choice. One can serve other souls in energy form in Heaven. It takes longer to erase debt in Heaven. The Earth-school is tough and gives you many opportunities to polish your soul. On Earth, time is measured, and matter is heavy. The All of Heaven is free and open, joyous and harmonious. We would not ever choose to leave such a perfect and comfortable place without the divine desire to abide by the paramount law of righting wrongs. You are always growing with many helpers at your service no matter where you choose to be.

REMEMBER . . .

- Hell is an idea of control.
- We give ourselves every chance to improve.
- You are your own judge.

- You have lived many times before.

- Unconditional love recognizes the best in everyone.

- Many evils have been done in the name of religion.

- You think like your group and you can change your thinking.

- You have all the time you need.

- Souls are at every level of learning.

- Imbalance can cause dis-ease.

- There is a divine desire to right wrongs.

Chapter 10

Life on Earth

The Descent

What are the steps you take when you plan a vacation, a new experience, or something different from your everyday life? First, you think of what you want to do. Then, you think of where you want to do it and who you want to come with you. Your trip is planned around what you might want to experience while away. If you want to go mountain climbing, you invite people with like skills and interests to accompany you, or with a beginner to teach. You decide which mountains you wish to climb. You look at a map to help you decide and plan how to get there. You choose whether to drive, fly, take a bus, train, or boat, and what route to take. You pack up everything you will need—boots, foods, hiking gear, tents, and supplies. You don't want to be without the things you need most or the trip will be more difficult. You may save up money a long time to make the trip, anticipating your plans. Or the timing might be right to go with your friends and you take the money out of your savings to take off on your adventure. Either way, you think before you go. You may consult friends, too, getting their advice on a place to go and enjoyable things to do there, so you can get the most out of your trip. You decide when you will return home and how.

After you have climbed the mountain, explored a new city, lounged on a beach, gone on an exploratory trip, visited old friends, toured great sites and museums, or cruised the oceans, it is always good to return home to your base where all your stuff is and where you are most comfortable. Then, once you are home, you have the memories and pictures of your trip to share with everyone. It was uniquely your experience. As one often says in telling a story, "You had to be there." You can't quite describe the whole experience. You tell everyone about your trip and then as time goes on, the memory of it fades little by little. There are parts of it, and people you met, that are not forgotten. But mostly, you recall the adventures through your photographs or relive them in conversations with those who were with you.

After a while, you decide to go on another trip somewhere else. Maybe with other people this time. Of course, every vacation is not wonderful. Often, bad weather, rough roads, unexpected delays, detours, crowds, or acts of nature can get in the way of a smooth trip. This is just the way it is.

On a vast and wondrous scale in creating, evolving, and re-creating, this is what you have done many times. You were comfortably at Home, in Heaven the All, and thought, "I want a new experience. I desire to grow and learn." So, you think about where you have already been and decide where you'd like to go now. You take out the map of the Universe and say, "Well, the Earth-school planet has many opportunities for learning. I think I'll go there again and fix up what I screwed up before, or help 'so and so' through their experience, or be of service to my fellow souls, or just enjoy myself with all the good energy I've stored up." Going away from the All is always a risk, but nothing ventured, nothing gained!

You meet with some friends, the record keepers or travel agents, and create a life plan. You select a composite personality needed in this life to accomplish all you wish. If you need to be a leader, you choose aspects of intelligence, forcefulness, and assurance that the personality will need. If you are going to be a father with many children, you select aspects of experiences from your past to help you be a father. If you need to be a sturdy, hard worker to provide for others, you may choose personality traits to help you carry this through. Perhaps you tell the record keepers, "I'd like to go to Kansas and be a male and join my friend, Bob, the one I cheated in Africa last life-time—so I can make it up to him. I also need to be with the soul energies, Sally, for my mom, and Fred for my dad, because we three have had conflicts in the past. This would be a good opportunity for us to work on this together in a family situation. Then, the energy, Sam, has agreed to be my brother this time around, as he is a soul mate and we built pyramids in Egypt together a long time ago. I owe him some loyalty and respect. I also want to make sure Alice is available to make this trip, and play a part in my life somehow, as she is a good teacher. I'd like to learn from her. And I have a group karma to fix with Tom, Dick, Harry, and Mabel, so the timing is right for me to be their father to work on this. Fran is planning this trip with me and has agreed again to be my mate, my wife, and to bring the children into our lives. We have been married many times before and other times, I have been female and she has been male so we could experience that type of energy flow."

It takes great planning with all these souls to organize a lifetime together. Some may not be available or have their own ideas about what they need to do—even changing their mind at the last minute. There are travel guides who may advise you about situations you are setting up, but the final choice is always yours. Sometimes, you can bite off more than you can chew. If everyone can make it, you plot out who goes first and where. You agree to fulfill obligations in this lifetime experience together.

This can be very complicated. Remember, each of these souls also has their own plan and contacts. They each have their own soul growth situations and relationships to set up. Each soul also has the right to alter choices along the way. All are responsible for their choices.

Okay, so you know where you are going and who is going along. Now you pack for the trip. You need energies of all forms to have with you while you are away. So you go to the bank of your energies and the All and set up an energy payment plan for the length of your trip. One day. Three years. Twenty-four years. Fifty-two years. Seventy-seven years. One hundred and two years. How much are you going to need, and when on this life road are you going to need more or less? You check the universal energies, astrology, for a time to be born on planet Earth. Certain months of the year will avail energies to you for the development of your personality and characteristics. You select them. When you, as a baby, breathe in your first Earth energies, you set in motion a constant flow from the "bank." The ignition on the car is turned, and the trip has begun. The soul has begun its life path.

First, your parents went before you and were born into their selected time. If all goes according to plan, along comes the opportunity for you to design the physical body you need to fulfill all you desire in this life. All is dependent on others' "right use" of energy, and souls following their "higher" direction and intuition. You select your parents and the circumstances in which to launch your early development, which will help you adjust to being in a physical body on Earth. Always, no matter the most wonderful or dire situation, there is something being learned. Keep in mind that everyone is working on something. There is always a lot going on. There is give and take and decisions being made, left and right. Ideas are flying and circumstances are endlessly created.

It's really all quite amazing, and is a wonder it works as well as it does. An overall divine order prevails that you helped set up. That is, all energy is good. If you misuse it, you must be responsible for it and correct it. Life on Earth, though, is not just about correcting past mistakes; it allows souls to use their energy to celebrate everyone's creation and all its beauty. The soul energy is first, last, and always. All the encounters with other souls and their personalities, and the physical stuff of the Earth, can complicate the trip experience.

Birth

The time is right. You know where and when you are leaving. So, you begin tinkering on your vehicle, the design of your body. You build what you need. Your mom is pregnant, and you watch the physical development of your new body. You decide the sex, height, body build, eye, hair, and skin colors, and design your mental abilities and talents. You watch from Home and wait. You can read your mother's emotions. A soul knows if it is wanted or not. Sometimes, the mother is in great distress and the soul coming in can't tell what the mother will do.

The soul at Home is free to the entire Universe and is a being of light and power. If all goes according to plan, the soul moves down from its higher self and settles into the fetus. Now that it has entered a body, it will be cramped up for four to six months. Some souls enter at three months, but most don't enter until five months, as this is a very long time to be so confined after one has been completely free. One must be careful not to contribute to the disruption of the life path of another. A fetus is not yet on its life path. Not until a baby is outside the mother and takes its first breath does it pull in the energies for its life plan. A mother should decide if she wants this life before the soul settles into the body. Very few souls want to experience abortion. When a soul can read the mother's emotions, and if this is her intent, then it might leave the body early since it knows it won't be able to fulfill its plan. Sometimes, a mother's emotions are too changing and the soul coming in can't tell what will happen. He or she gets caught and experiences the abortion. Other times, in normal situations and with an emotionally healthy mother, the soul may make a last minute choice not to begin the life it had planned, which results in a full-term baby being stillborn. If the baby fulfills its plan and is born, it accepts the energies for its life path on its first breath.

Ideally, labor should not be induced. The soul chooses the time of its birth for the universal energies that will be available for its life path. A child born not at the time of their choosing might have a difficult adjustment later because it has been forced to use different energies.

Science today is marvelous and men and women have learned how to manipulate creative energies. They can now offer couples that have medical problems the opportunity to conceive. Also, women can choose sperm and bypass a mate and bring forth a child on her own. Everyone has the right to these choices. The word cloning sends shivers through the minds of many. Just remember that all of us have been experimenting with creation since the day we saw the light! If a soul chooses to enter a body that was cloned, being perfect or imperfect, it has made this choice for their own soul evolvement. Souls do not have to enter any body form they do not wish to enter. Even if you are cloned, the clone is a separate soul with its own complete experiences and agenda.

No one else, ever, is just like you. Yes, there is always a chance for misuse in playing with the human form. It has been done before and will continue, as mankind learns differently, at his pace, how he would want to be created. To be born on Earth, we move away from our Home and source of understanding and freedom. Sometimes, in various faiths, it is called the "sin" of separation or an "original sin." Actually, it is the original idea of the ultimate desire to experience the use of power to create. The farther away from Home one gets, the more this original idea is forgotten. Sometimes, people get way off their paths and the farther off they get, the harder it is to get back on track. It is harder to remember the original idea of who you are. The energy of Home is always there. It is a good thing to attend churches and services and meetings of like spiritual minds, as they help to remind us who we are—spirit first.

It is difficult to have a birth memory because it is often a fearful and traumatic experience for the soul. After all, at Home, you are your own true self and are omnipotent (have unlimited power), being a part of the God or All force. And now, your energy is trapped in a body and does not have total freedom. It has lost control and is at the mercy of others and the elements. It's no wonder you cry when you take your first breath. It is often not a good memory, though it is a memory, subconsciously. Some people, with the right person's help, and for the right reasons, can be regressed to their birth experience and re-capture coming forth into light and love.

Some babies have a tremendous amount of strength to hold onto the soul energy and be born with AIDS, deformities, or addictions. These souls are highly evolved and have chosen this experience to teach others. It is a sacrifice made for mankind. Babies given up for adoption often take advantage of a vehicle, the mother, to get to the Earth. Before they leave Home, they know the biological parents will not be the everyday parents to raise them. Maybe the biological parents are fulfilling karma by conceiving, giving birth and then giving the baby up to others. Often, adopted children want to contact the original energy to thank them for their input.

The baby comes into the light on the Earth and, hopefully, into loving and wanting arms. It is a very joyous time if the baby is well-loved and taken care of. The soul energy and life force that energizes it has given up quite a lot to get to this place. This baby has a mission, a purpose, and a plan. You chose your parents, family, circumstances, country, and continent. You even chose your name, birth date, and numerology, to give yourself the right vibrations for the sound of your name and the energies that each letter and number represents. If Mom and Dad didn't pick up on your pre-birth message, you probably don't like your name and may change it. Or, the name is correct and you are fighting its energies.

Now that you are here and have reached your destination, you have a lot to do. First, you have to get used to this body you made, and the weight, sights, and sounds of the Earth-school. Some new babies decide not to stay long. Perhaps the body doesn't work right. Or maybe the situation is too difficult for it to begin and complete its plan. Or, the baby could have planned a very brief time with parents and family, to teach them a lesson of love, receiving, grieving, and releasing. You don't ever know for sure, but for sure, something is going on.

To come to the Earth to live is a wonderful decision. You have said to yourself, "I want the opportunity to be my best. I want to experience my fellow souls and all our creations. I give myself the chance to right any wrongs, learn from others, gain new growth, and have fun."

Remember, you left loved ones at Home who are looking out for you, as well as your own storehouse of energy that is your higher self. As the Earth baby grows, the higher self is very quiet in order to allow the personality to develop in the new and rapidly growing body.

Childhood

The ideal is, of course, that each baby born is wanted and revered. That the family welcoming the child focuses completely on this new soul's every need. Oh my, just think if everyone were truly aware that when a new baby arrives, it chose its parents and family as the group to serve, teach, learn from, or just enjoy. Babies, by design, are beautiful, sweet, and soft. They are the most helpless creatures born on the Earth, totally dependent on others to survive. Bringing a soul to Earth is a tremendous responsibility. If the parents have had what they themselves needed, and have been well cared for, they are more likely to be good parents. People learn how to treat others from how they have been treated. But all the same, souls choose parents and families and situations of all types. Souls search out the situation they need to experience in order to learn and understand energy use.

A soul needs to be well rounded, so chooses to be in the male or female body form. One may be a male time after time, and then choose to be female to experience all the things and feelings of being female. Chances are, all the men out there have been women and vice versa. So before you criticize behavior, know that you, too, have been in the other body type. This thought should, hopefully, make you hesitate before taking any superior attitude over another group.

The new child on Earth is quickly plunged into the material world. He or she may have everything or nothing. It is quickly learned that to have what you need is more fun and comfortable. Well, not only for the child, but also for everyone. Children have the right to develop in a safe and healthy environment. They need to be protected and taught about the physical world, as well as the spiritual world. It begins with the very first time the parent says, "No!" The rules begin. Values are set. Moral guidelines are learned. The child begins to make choices.

Picture a newborn baby's mind as a blackboard, the chalk and eraser sitting just so on its sill. Every sound, idea, treatment, impression, perception, shadow, and thought is, moment by moment, written on the blackboard. The brain is storing more and more information as the child grows. Wow, this is one big blackboard! It is as large or small as it needs to be. The chalk never wears out. What is written becomes the child's language and beliefs. It also becomes the life's recording and history. When the soul is a child, the family does the writing. If a child is taught that a chair is a chair, the picture of a chair and the word "chair" is eventually written on the blackboard. If the child is shown a chair and then is told that the chair is a lamp, then the child has on his blackboard, in his mind, this identification. This is not correct, of course, but until "lamp" is erased and corrected with "chair," this is what the child will know and believe.

The responsibility of the family is enormous, to write on the child's blackboard mind the right labels and identifications. Even if they are near perfect and careful at doing this, the child's mind can perceive information individual to its soul's needs.

The early years are a "free" time, without consequences of debt, until children have gained enough information about their new location. Bonds with others are built, language is learned, and the personality needed for this life is developed. Some bloom early, some later, depending on the plan. The rules of living with fellow souls are learned. At an early age, the child knows "Yes" and "No." It also knows that to do a "No," means consequences. When a "Yes" is done, usually good things happen. They learn right from wrong.

Little by little, the child sees that his life impacts others. He can't do what he wants, when he wants. The child has an empty blackboard for filling up, remember? There is so much to record. Choices are made from which to pick and choose. "I can use this." "I don't want this." Often, what others see as a bad choice may be a good choice for a soul. Choices are made at the higher level as well. The soul may choose to be with a certain person, have an illness, or be in a particular situation to learn from that experience. If that choice impacts you, then maybe you are meant to learn something, too!

A horrible parent, who beats a child and is cruel, may just be the example the child chose so as not to be that kind of a parent himself. To be a neglected child could be a type of rejection the soul chose to experience because perhaps they inflicted this treatment on a child in a previous life. To bring a child to Earth that is mentally deficient, physically challenged, or difficult, may be a soul's chance to repay a prejudice, a great fear, or a deep lack of understanding of this experience.

A child may choose to repeat a parent's lesson and act as an example of good parenting or lousy parenting. However, a parent is not the only teacher. Every fellow soul with whom one comes into contact has the ability to teach. The simplest sentence or a casual look from a stranger can teach a lesson. Even in silence, what is not said or done, there is energy from which to learn. Remember, everyone came together on Earth for the same purpose and with the same goal. Try to be patient, and begin with understanding yourself. Enjoy the opportunities in the trip!

When you go on a vacation for a week or so, usually by the second day you are away, you forget the lawn at home, the crabby neighbors, the bills, the schedule at your job, the leaky faucet, and your list of things "to do." You get into your new location and what you are doing. You figure out where places are, meet new faces, and enjoy new personalities. You are all on vacation, so you have this in common. Your focus is on where you are now, what you are doing, and with whom. When someone says, "Where are you from and what do you do?" you recall this information of your life and share it. The longer you are away, the less clear the details of your life back home become. On vacation, you don't take all your clothes, or the details of your job and house. You don't take everyone you know, or all your money. You take what you need for the duration of the trip and always know that, if you run out of money, or left something at home, you can send for it.

When one has a strong drawing to a place, or person, style, group, era, or civilization, it is often because they have been there, done that, or know the person. There is a reason. This is either a flicker of a memory or guidance to be where and with whom you need to be in order to get on with your life path.

The baby on Earth is fully engrossed in this new life. It does not bring the memory of every life it has ever experienced, or all its energy. It cannot use the memories of every past life, and the details and reasons for choices in them. The baby's focus is on now and the plan it set up this time. If it wasn't this way, a lot of energy would go into holding on to people, places, and things, and the ideas from past lives would be a burden and hindrance to new achievements.

Sometimes, if an adult asks a young child, "Where are you from, or what did you do before you came here?" a child will respond with memories from a past life, maybe a name or some experience. They remember, but they soon forget, as their new life gets busier. Other children, often referred to as "child prodigies," choose to recall past accumulated discoveries, talents, or gifts, and display them shockingly to adults. They may be science whizzes, musical, or "old for their age." It seems amazing. They chose to spend their time on Earth using what they already knew to learn more and to go forward. They pick parents and an environment to support them. Often, they are souls with much experience and have come to serve their fellow men.

Some babies come with buddies! They are twins, triplets, quads, quints, or sextuplets. These choices can be multifaceted. Deep and loving past experiences can motivate souls to want to experience, together and very closely, the same situation and parents. They could have a karmic relationship that needs to be worked out and the best way to do it is from birth on. Or they may select to be born together to spend the early years very close to work off a debt, and then separate to improve their individual spiritual growth. There can also be a mission for this team of two, three, four, five, or six or more, to be raised in the same environment and, in time, contribute to mankind's store of knowledge. Remember, there is always a lot going on and you don't know what it is, so it is always best not to judge.

A more severe situation of multiple births is when the souls' bodies are conjoined; they are sometimes called Siamese twins. These souls could have had an intense love or hate for one another in a past life and chose this body form to work it out. If you hated someone so fiercely, what a tremendous task to eradicate the energy of hate by being attached to them, forced to know their every move and function and to share a lifetime being physically one with them. This is extremely rare, and a very difficult life to live. Even though having conjoined children is heartbreaking for a family, remember that the souls did not have to enter the baby body. And should one child be sacrificed for the sake of the other, this is their plan, too. Medical science has been able to separate some conjoined children. The separation may or may not have been part of the plan. Remember that other people's ideas often interfere with other's plans. Staying the course is often difficult. Multiple births usually feel a great loss of self when the one they shared such a close life with goes Home. As hard as it is, they will reunite at Home, as everyone will.

The pain for parents is monstrous, but they should remember that they gave these souls an opportunity to express their creativity and, perhaps, to gain great soul growth in being who they were and teaching the family hard and lasting lessons.

Autistic and Down syndrome children also choose their parents, and are teachers living a limited lifetime. Much debt can be erased in these life expressions. Often, one parent cannot handle the everyday care of one of these children. It simply may not be theirs to do, or they do not accept the challenge of the lessons they set up. Or the child goes to others for the lifetime. The parent will choose another opportunity, if it is necessary for their soul growth. To people not in it, this rejection of a "duty" is looked upon as unforgivable. But the fact is, you do not know what is going on. Often, the parent does not either. There is a strong urge to do it or not. Each charts his or her path. Whatever creative energy decided this body form, the souls and families put themselves in this situation to learn and teach others.

Genetic diseases are also chosen to work with and learn from. Sometimes, a baby chooses a genetic disease and leaves the Earth to follow their plan. This is devastating for the family, after so much anticipation and love. But it is a choice that is often made. Something is always learned. The parents and family may be tested in their closeness, character, and compassion. They learn more about one another in these sad circumstances. Some families are motivated to create a group or organization to help others in similar circumstances. This is taking a difficult situation and re-creating it into a positive energy. It not only helps others in this situation, but also energizes the founders of the organization to go forward. Maybe one soul made a sacrifice to teach many.

The Teen Years

So here you are, a teenager. Beautiful you! You are in your youth, blooming all over the place. You couldn't wait to become a teenager so you could do more and have more freedom. But what you have found out is that everyone is cautious of "the teenager." Everyone is watching you and you're watching all of your friends to see how they are handling this emotionally clumsy time.

Up until now, you were this adorable kid. If you had a somewhat normal childhood, you might have enjoyed being with your family and doing things with them. These people were your security. You chose your parents and siblings to build the foundation for your whole life.

The problem is that when you are a teenager, you often can't see beyond tomorrow and feel that everything that happens NOW is of utmost, piercing importance NOW! And your body is not cooperating. Chemical changes and physical growth spurts are distracting, and personal, and sometimes painful. Just when you "may" finally look like the person you admire the most, acne attacks! Nothing quite goes the way you want. However, these years are the epitome of your physical growth on Earth and your body is stretching to its final height. Your intelligence is being taught and tested and tapped. Your emotions are all over the place.

Just when your parents think that they can enjoy all their hard work and protection they provided for you, YOU become a screaming, debating, carefree, daredevil! And, of course, NO ONE understands you AT ALL!

Your friends become your guidance system. This is because they have chosen to be born into the same timeframe of life as you. You are all essentially a very big group consciousness that will design and develop the values, scope, and depths of your generation. So, you want to be LIKE all your friends, as did your parents and grandparents. Sometimes they just forget this. Hence, you don't think they UNDERSTAND you. But, in their "day," they, too, wanted to be accepted and they, too, didn't think that their parents understood them. These are the cycles of growth on Earth.

The baby held its head up, rolled over, crawled, walked, skipped, ran, and soaked up billions of pieces of information to speak its language. A day came when the child realized IT WAS ALIVE! The thought process recognized that the being you are thinks and has power to make things happen! Actually, the child, from birth, makes things happen every moment of every day. The new energy that this baby is demands total care to survive and, in a normal family, becomes the center of the Universe.

Most children are pretty happy until they learn the word "NO" and the consequences of their actions. All of a sudden, it seems that the center of the Universe is now expected to change its thinking and consider everyone else in the Universe. The teen years can be a battle of wills between the parents, teachers, and the teenager. This is the time when the soul begins to pick up its karmic package. When one begins to work on things, they need to improve their use of energies. Some may take a short time to learn; others may last a lifetime.

The karmic package is the list of items you drew up with the travel agents after reviewing your previous lives. It might say: I must learn to forgive. I must learn to speak kindly. I must know what it is to be in need. I owe a woman respect. I need to learn to handle money. I must not fear water. I need to develop a more loving personality. I need to temper a violent streak I have shown in past lives. I must experience betrayal. I need to love myself. A vast variety of possibilities pertinent to each soul's lifetime are contained in the karmic package.

Remember, the teenager chose its parents. If there is a battle with one or both, perhaps whatever needed to be worked out, learned, and resolved from past lives has begun. Not all children feel a bond with one or both parents. What is going on here? It is hard to say. The souls involved are not together by mistake. Maybe they are learning patience, understanding, or reaping what has been sown. Every family is different.

Parents in anguish over a teenager's behavior might ask, what is going on here? Maybe a very strong-willed child is practicing its strength and weaknesses in a safe environment of love, because its soul knows its life plan is going to be tough and it will need these experiences to learn and survive in adult life.

Maybe the parents were weak, unloving, or ineffectual parents in a previous life and they are getting the chance to correct and learn a better way. Or, maybe they were testy teenagers who could not previously express themselves, were dominated, or undisciplined, and this is a chance for them to reach out and learn to connect with a teenager as the parents.

For every life, there is a reason and a story as to why they are with one person or another. To be sure, if you took responsibility for a new life and did not care for it well, you will be the uncared for child sometime to KNOW what this is like and to understand. The life may have to be repeated with the same souls involved to repay a misuse.

The teenager is walking across a high wire from childhood to adulthood. They are trying not to fall off, trying to keep their eyes ahead, on the future, not looking down or back. Forward is the only way to go. But staying on that wobbly wire, one step at a time is very difficult. The time seems endless and the anxiety to get over to the adult side is high. Not only the teenager feels this. The parents are walking their own high wire in fretful steps along with them. However, this is never really known until the teenager is a parent and walks this wire *with* their teenager.

Teenagers generally think that they know everything. This is necessary to launch them forward with confidence. They also feel immortal, as their bodies are at the epitome of strength, performance, and beauty. It is a good thing that these parts of the whole are in place, as the emotions are usually a tornado of scattered energy, trying to catch up with fears of the future, deep desires for acceptance, and a developing self-image. If the teen knew that this is all normal and that all these new problems that seem to be in their lives "all of a sudden," are of their own design for their soul growth, how much easier it would be to sort out all the aches, pains, and feelings.

Many important choices are made during the teen years. What to study? Who to hang out with? Who to love? The physical body is bursting to express its sexual urges. And in all of this, the world has become bigger. And driving a car grants one more freedom. It is a wild time and an instant decision can alter one's entire life path. Of course, maybe this is your life path. Only you know. If you set up a difficult obstacle course in life, then you are challenging yourself to experience many different situations to learn from and overcome.

Teenagers would be wise to look around and see how others live and the consequences of their choices. Every soul on Earth is here for all others, even if only to serve as an example. This is a hard thing for some teens to do. If they don't, or can't, it is because they are set on their path and must do what they must do.

Parents often blame themselves when the best-laid wishes for their children's lives go awry. This is especially true if they had to learn the hard way when they were teenagers. All good teachers and parents want the best for their children. But sometimes, the choices made are not "personal" to the parents. It is just the way the child must go, no matter the parent's input. The best all can hope for is that everyone learns and loves more through all the hills and dales of a loved one's life. Sometimes, it is very hard to do. Being flexible, positive, and spiritual is a constant goal.

Just as the baby and school child change and develop, so at

last does the teenager. In a good situation, there is growing up time and an introduction to the world in self-sufficiency and contribution. Hopefully, the young adults take their places in the world, open and embracing everything new, and loving the process of learning. Then they, too, will share their experience and soul knowledge with another generation.

But all souls are at a different place in experience and learning. The damaged child may have chosen this experience, or is a victim of another's misuse of energy. Everyone, no matter where they are on their path, must recognize and make an effort to uplift another in love, because they are a part of us. A soul of many life experiences knows there is a reason for every soul's circumstances. Dharma, good use of energy, piles up in your energy bank and benefits your deeper understanding and the ultimate, unconditional love.

Interestingly, the teen years are often remembered fondly, even if they were tumultuous. This is because souls don't forget an awakening, or the first steps of a long journey. Building a foundation is always exciting since it is what we will stand upon our whole life. It's a good thing that it is possible to look back with family and friends who were there with you, to share the memories and to reinforce the foundation.

Take heart if you are a teenager reading this, or a parent in the grip of worry over your tattooed, pierced, pink-haired, indifferent child. Things always change: you or them, or both. The teen is on the path you brought them into, as you are on yours, watching and guiding them.

REMEMBER . . .

- Take what energies you need to the Earth-school.
- Plan your lifetime itinerary.
- Design your body and circumstances.

- Abortion, still birth, and cloning are all choices.
- Some souls are in service to teach.
- The body grows; the personality develops.
- Childhood is rapid learning and adjustment to the Earth.
- Fill the blackboard mind with information.
- The child's life impacts others.
- Karmic and soul mate bonding.
- Teenager steps on the long life path.
- For every life there is a story and a reason.
- All things change.

Chapter 11
Personality and Energy

Personality is an expression of one's soul. You design your personality to serve your Earth experience needs. It is easy to get caught up in the personality and the wants and desires of stuff on the Earth. Now, let me tell you, here and now, that the Earth you created is a beautiful place. You should, if it is in your plan, try and see as much of it as you can. Your lifetime on Earth is supposed to be joyous. After all, you are joining old friends on an adventurous "vacation" to explore and learn new things. It is an opportunity to get it right, to clean up your act! You need to be brave and draw on who you really are every day, and ask your buddies at Home to help guide you and send you strength or energy to do your best. Your higher self at Home is all thought energy. It does not have a physical body and emotions; therefore, there is no need for a personality. The person has the personality. One's emotions respond to some thought or action. Is it a negative or positive reaction? Right use or misuse? One can choose to accept or reject forms of energy from others—to react or not react.

Each soul is a Universe within itself. Now what in the world does this mean, you say? Each soul, even multiple birth souls, have had and are having different experiences and perceptions of what goes on around them and what happens to them and the choices they make. So each and every one is truly unique. By your own design, you are where you are today. If you don't like it, change it. It you can't change it now, for a hundred and fourteen reasons, then ask yourself, "What am I learning in this situation? Is there something I need to do differently? Do I feel compelled to finish something up with a person or group?" Can you imagine a future plan of who you want to be, how, with whom, and why? Do you have an urge to accomplish something? Does your conscience, your higher self, tell you to right a wrong? You know these things as no one else does. There are many helpers around you to help you think on these things, so you can make positive decisions. There are many ways to right wrongs—not always in like kind or to the same person. Religions are clubs that think like you do. Since day one, the soul in physical form has looked "up" and beyond itself for answers and a source. You are your own source! It is all there at your disposal. We created rules in our religions and philosophies to give us ways to connect to our own answers and guidelines. Whether you pray in church, meditate, or kneel and face Mecca, it is an action to remind yourself that you are more than an Earthly being. All beliefs and religions are not on the same wavelength. Where there is good and right use, there is misuse. In the name of some "religions," there are people who wish to control others for the gratification of their personality. Those who are controlled allow it. They are often wavering souls who are searching and need firm guidelines to live by. These groups often set themselves aside, which causes others to fear their intent. It is best to let them be, as they are on a path of choice. It is just different from yours.

Mankind is comfortable with those like themselves—those who live alike, look alike, dress alike, think alike, and worship alike. Yet, you are all one energy and one mind. The goal is to expand your thinking to embrace all life forms, as you embrace and accept yourself.

It is said that the twenty-first century is the information age, meaning that more information is easily available to man. But the choice of what you do with the information is the same.

Will it be used for a rightful purpose, or to take advantage of and misuse others?

Technology should bring fellow souls closer together. It was designed for this. One can now see on a screen how others live in Turkey, Africa, South America, Cuba, China, Russia, Pango Pango, and the USA. One can also see what one group of people can do to another—positive or negative.

Everyone is not living an "equal" lifestyle, because men and women created different situations to experience and from which to learn. You may get up in the morning and turn on your computer to send e-mail to your sister in Japan. Another may get up and start walking to go see a sister in a village fifty miles away to keep in touch. Each person experiences and evolves in his or her own time. You may be on your last lifetime on Earth, wrapping up loose ends and testing out many lessons learned over eons. Or you may be a young soul carefully starting out. You may be a teacher of others, or the student. No book could contain the listings of variables possible that were created by choices over time by every soul.

You are all equal in spirit. Remember, you are all from the same energy and one mind, always and forever. Your personality is your unique expression. You need to be quiet and think, to get your guidance, and use all the wonders on the Earth you created to keep moving forward in balance and with the best energy ever—love.

Personalities are how people express themselves and are defined. She's shy. He's boastful. She's a nut. He's a jerk. He's funny. She's sweet. He's a creep. She's a liar. I trust him. I don't trust her. He is easy to be with. She's a pain to take anywhere. You get the idea.

We recognize not only the physical form and the sound of a voice, but also the energy of a person. You are drawn to some people because you love their energy. They help you to feel good, think good, or be good. They share their energy with you—you receive it and enjoy it. Other people that you meet repel you with their energy because they project hurtful, mean, or thoughtless energy. Your energy and theirs do not blend. You must work to be with them or near them. It usually exhausts your energy, as they are sapping it from you. Your soul and spirit has an acceptance of what is. It knows, and is not burdened by material influences, such as money, sex, and stuff to exchange. One's personality expressed by words, actions, and reactions is a composite of thousands and thousands of inputs from experiences, created through your everlasting soul's travels in lifetimes. There are people who train on the Earth to help people to see how they are using their energy through their personality. Religion is the physical world's school of soul guidance. Spirituality is the building that houses all the beliefs and religions.

So, where are you now in all of these thoughts? Try not to dismiss an idea because it is new or different. The personality likes to tell the thinking mind what to think. The mind is the first control of the personality. Sometimes, the mind is overridden by a personality that has taken over. When something, anything, is uncomfortable and "doesn't seem to fit," the personality almost always rejects anything new.

When you are in the flow of your energy, you know it and feel the fulfillment of it. There is a sense of comfort when you are in your flow. You can handle all kinds of things that happen. The personality never takes control. The energy is accepted and used. When you are in the flow, it doesn't repeat itself. It is constantly changing and you are flowing with the changes.

Have you bumped up against someone who isn't in the flow? They are usually unhappy and have scattered energies. Your compassionate self wants to help, as you may have a clear vision of what they need to do, or can see their actions being repeated over and over. Each fellow man and woman has a responsibility to help, to teach, and then to step back and allow others to use their own energies. When you teach a child to balance on a two-wheel bicycle, you don't ride around on the bike going, "See how this is done?" No, you put them on the bike, with their own energy, and teach them how to steer and balance. Then you let go, so they can do it on their own. It would slow the rider down to allow you to hold on. They would become dependent on your energy to move them on the bike. Then, they still haven't learned and you are exhausted!

Women and men try so hard to change one another's energies. This is not good and besides, how can you? How can others change you? Soul growth is a slow process. It involves much trial and error, falling down and getting up and starting over. Man has every chance he needs to restart and try again!

If you play it safe all the time, how can you grow? One must retrain one's thinking. Even if at first you say to yourself, "Okay, my first reaction is no." Then think, is it always negative? Try to say to yourself, "Let me keep this new idea in mind, and toss it around a few days. I'll see if I can get used to it and maybe use it, or see a different perspective." Then, if after this little leeway you give yourself, you just can't embrace the new idea, then don't. The time is not right. It is okay. However, if a little part of you thinks, "I may explore this idea further, or accept this new person (plan, setback, confusion)," then, do so in baby steps. It is hard to do. The desire to make the effort means the time is right for you. As you know well from your experiences in living on Earth, everyone does not think, act, or believe in the same way. Everyone is just trying to live their life the best they can. It would just be so easy to say: I can't change myself. I can't change things. It's all his or her fault. It's the government's fault. It's the weather's fault. The devil made me do it. Or, God let this happen.

You really know better! You know that you are a part of something GREAT. Not only a part of it, but a co-creator of it. When you were born on the Earth-school, you came with a new and fresh blackboard of a mind, as if from a factory. Along with your blackboard mind came a lifetime supply of chalk and a very important tool, the eraser!

Your fellow souls and you in the All decided that everyone would have every opportunity to continue to be their best. No matter how stupid, wrong, awful, crazy, foolish, or mean a soul may choose to act, it always has the opportunity to fix, repair, correct, delete, reboot, and refresh all the misuses of energy. Now, isn't this wonderful? And, my dearest, striving soul on Earth, it is true! You can take it to the bank (of energy)!

You are the All, the God, the Father, the Mother. You are made up of all good. So you've made a few mistakes? Think of the person who is the absolutely most precious to you. The one you care about and love the most. The one you would give your blood, an eye, a kidney, a piece of your liver to. The one you want most to be happy, safe, and secure. The one you would protect with your very life. Do you have her or him in mind? Now, look in a mirror. The very same is due you.

What the other guy or gal is, you have been or will be yourself. Now this is scary! But the things you can't stand and dislike in others are either the very things you have already worked so hard to correct and perfect, or the things you need to work on yet! Or, you would not have such a reaction of even thinking of feeling "dislike."

You have heard of "bad" people turning their entire lives around and taking an entirely new direction in positive thinking and action. These are fellow souls who erased entire paragraphs of thoughts on their blackboard and rewrote better ones! What you put on the blackboard stays on the blackboard, until you erase it. It is your story, your design, your domain, and your soul evolvement. You and you alone create it, evaluate it, and redo it. You cannot, nor do you have the right to, pick up another's eraser, or judge what's on their blackboard just as they do not have the right to interfere with yours.

REMEMBER . . .

- Personality is the expression of one's soul.
- Life on Earth should be joyous.
- Emotions respond.
- Each soul is one-of-a-kind forever and always.
- You are who you are by your own design.
- You are your own source of answers. Think.
- Your personality defines you.
- Don't let your personality control you.
- Be comfortable in the flow of positive energy.
- Others can't change you so how can you change others?

Chapter 12

Discovering Who You Are

You have chosen a life situation to experience on Earth at a time when the planet is very populated—currently about six billion souls. The reason for so many souls here now is not because your travel agents said, "Have I got a deal for you! For half price, you can all go to Earth and have some great experiences." What happened is that two other planets to which souls would travel for growth and experience became unavailable. Souls who would have chosen them decided on this planet instead. Earth is not the "baby" planet and does have a lot of niches to offer everyone, from the primitive to the advanced learner experience. Many souls also took the opportunity to come to Earth to gain soul growth before an expected cataclysmic event (see chapter on Shifting the Shift) created a vast chasm of time with far fewer bodies available to live in on Earth.

For these reasons, Earth became the "vacation hotspot" and therefore is more populated than it has ever been in the history of the planet. Where were you before you chose Earth? Did you get bumped from going to another galaxy? It's a good thing that everyone is from the same source. This conglomeration of experiences and creativity is a glorious mingling opportunity.

Could the number of more "advanced learner" souls now on Earth account for the many technological leaps in the last hundred years? This is a fun thought to chew on—a meshing of many ideas from boundless and limitless pools of knowledge.

But many are not a part of your path. Ages ago, the populations were small. There were fewer souls with whom to cross paths. Now, there are so many chances to touch other lives. This can be overwhelming, so you must ask yourself if this or that person is essential to your plan. You cannot do something about every situation. When you are not directly a part of a world condition, it is not your responsibility.

You have many connections and have responsibilities to them. By age twenty, the intellect has written vast amounts of information on the blackboard. Some may get the eraser out and think, "I don't like this anymore!" Or, "I'm not doing this another time." A lot will be erased and rewritten as each soul experiences life on Earth. The energy of the soul feels forever strong and powerful. It is.

In the last half of the 1900s through today, young people have been encouraged to get an education before they married and had a family. This is always a good idea. Knowledge is power and enhances every life. At the same time, in the last quarter of the twentieth century, people have become more separated. Technology, along with good intentions, more mobility, and a desire by people for more comforts, has pulled people further apart. Often today, the time, nurturing, companionship, and conversation it takes to guide, comfort, and teach the young over the first twenty years of life is not expressed. This can lead to the need and desire for young people to be close to one another, and to capture what was lacking in the formative years. The need to be recognized, touched, listened to, and loved is a universal energy. Young people will become couples at a younger age due to their need for this experience to build upon. It is missing from their lives. They yearn for it.

There has also been (remember) a shift in energy from harmony through conflict to love through wisdom. These times now (2000s) are the new years of this energy flow. The new babies, the children from the 1970s forward, are harbingers of new thoughts and uses of expressions of positive energy.

The most perfect expression of energy is love. You know this! Well, actually you know all of this. I am just reminding you (I hope). Men and women are always in a state of looking for perfection. That is what we ARE. Through our choices, we have gotten away from this perfection and striving to learn and grow. We also look for guidelines and guides to make our theories into realities of what is lawful and unlawful.

There are souls on Earth that never give a thought as to why they are here, or what is after life on Earth and they don't care to explore this. Guess what? They are expressing, as they are capable at this time. Oftentimes, these folks lead simple lives in the physical world. They eat, sleep, work, play, make babies, and it is absolutely enough. It does not cross their mind as to why. Then, there are souls who spend most of their life in contemplation, study, and prayer to figure out what is going on. They sometimes wholly dedicate their energies to their fellow man.

Have you ever met someone who just doesn't have a clue? Perhaps they are even knowledgeable, but naïve and innocent in some ways. They could be the parts of us that are "baby souls" struggling in grown-up bodies and circumstances.

It is, for all, as it should be. Remember this. It will indeed make your life easier. You will see the odd, strange, young, old, yellow, red, bright, dull, loud, quiet, nasty, and holy, differently.

This is the desire of this book. As you see others more lovingly, they, too, will see you more lovingly. We can only hope! We, being your Angels, teachers, and guides watching out for you and sending love your way for clear vision and fulfillment of your life plan, as you need it to be.

Religions are good as they help to awaken your soul to your true self and purpose. It does not matter what others believe. They are where they are supposed to be. It is best to concern yourself with your own soul and what you have to learn.

Part of discovering who you are begins with the sex you chose. You needed to be masculine or feminine to fulfill your plan. Some souls go into great detail preparing their body makeup, chemistry, design, and personality. Others leave it up to the combination of their parents' egg and sperm. You may think, "This can't be! I wouldn't choose this or that!" But you did whether you chose specifically or not. You still made a choice. Get it?

Again, I remind you that All are one and the same. No matter if you eat snake for lunch, have a plate in your lip for fashion, believe cows are sacred, or desire the love of someone of your own sex.

After all, you only created on this planet two models of bodies to use while here. So why should you be surprised if the chemicals that you came up with, to have the bodies work this way or that, get blurred on occasion? On other galaxy systems, there are bodies created of more choices than male and female. Why not? All is possible. Thoughts are real things and are manifested. Just as Earth has balancing problems between males and females, this other place has its own set of problems. It happens. This is another thing for you to accept, because you recognize yourself in your fellow men and women.

Men, who like to wear women's clothes and act like women, may be this way due to a lack of firm definition between being male or female. The body is male, but the desire may be to experience a feminine life. Or, the male needs to express himself this way to fulfill some past misuse of masculinity or femininity.

Sometimes, some souls in female bodies would prefer to be

male and others in male bodies would rather be female. Both can be attracted to the energy of the same sex. There are millions of souls expressing themselves this way on the planet Earth-school. They are like you, learning and repaying debts owed to others in the way that they must. Be careful, and be kind now in your thinking. Some of these souls are experiencing this lifestyle because they were hateful and judgmental. They made no attempt to understand the homosexual exchange of energy. They now are experiencing it first hand, in a society that is struggling to understand. If you are not already accepting, be one who offers compassion toward this lifestyle. Thoughts are real things. It could be you. Watch what you write on your blackboard.

For many, this is as far off a thought as they can comprehend—as far off as the idea that there is a planet in the Universe that is almost entirely made of water, and that the souls who choose this experience live within it. It may be weird to your way of thinking, but it is true. And as above, so below: souls at Home also learn from new experiences.

Whenever you have a thought or feeling of repulsion for any of your fellow men and women's choices in life, STOP and think, "This could be me!" Or "What if it were me? How would I feel? React? Handle it?" In doing this, you connect with your higher self and remind yourself of who you really are. You save yourself a lot of grief in the (very) long run. This is not hard to do. It does take practice, as you are not allowing yourself to write on the blackboard a misuse toward one of your own kind, which would take twice as much energy to erase down the road.

Parents of physically and mentally challenged children, deaf or blind children, ill, misshapen children, or homosexual children, all suffer alike. With feelings of guilt and despair wrought out of love, the mind and heart yells, "It can't be! This is my child!" The parents naturally want to serve, protect, and teach their children well. To think that a soul in your care hurts or suffers because of its differences from the "normal" is a deep, deep pain. Great love from the mind and heart must surface and express acceptance of this soul who chose you, and whom you chose to bring to Earth. What a test and challenge! What an opportunity you all have designed and set up to become better and more loving souls. What a twist you put in the plot of your lives to work with, hurdle, fix, correct, and overcome in your story! It's not easy. There are aches, pains, fears, worries, expenses, and cruel opinions of others who don't yet understand. But you will teach them by who you are and how you react. If they don't "get it" now, they will one day, be sure.

We discover who we are by understanding others. All of this is an exchange of energy. Everything is energy. When you smile at another, shake hands, hug, speak, or make love, you are exchanging energy. All of the above (and everything not listed) can be done in the most loving and giving manner, or, it can be misused for negative and selfish motives. You certainly want credit for being loving. Well, you also get demerits for negative energy use. With all of this in mind, one cannot judge his fellow man for any use of any energy.

Yes, there are rules. And yes, everyone needs to help present them, show them, teach them, and preserve them. You don't want another to interfere with your choices. Remember, every soul is responsible for their use of their energy. On the big, planetary picture, everything each soul does affects all other souls. That is how you all got to the place in time you are now, reading this book!

Confucius, Buddha, Mohammed, Moses, Jesus, Gandhi, Martin Luther King, and Mother Theresa are the great teachers. All said, "Love one another." None specified love only the black, healthy, pretty, smart, rich, straight, non-littering, vegetarian, brown-eyed, or contributing souls. No, simply "love one another."

It is forgotten every day. We have reminders everywhere. Each soul is their own best reminder. Whoever you are, look into the mirror, deep into your own eyes, and listen to your conscience (the knowing). Be guided by your self. Need help? Just ask. When the student is ready and asks, the teacher and answers are provided. Be still and know that you are God/All.

Many roads lead to Home. There are many teachers and tools along the way to help you. You were no fool, coming to Earth without supplies and suppliers.

Humankind is intelligent, but also a slow learner. Each soul has to work through the material-matter world we created. You enslaved yourself in a body, and use your energy to do whatever you do for you personally. Technology has grown faster than man has evolved. Soul growth is a slow process, subtle and quiet. Too much intellect blocks out the energy of the soul. The more energy you put into the intellectual body, the harder the time you'll have "trying to figure it out." You need to take "it" higher for input and help.

REMEMBER . . .

- The number of people on Earth increases your chances to touch others' lives.
- You are learning and changing what's written on your blackboard.
- All yearn to be special to another.
- Everyone expresses what they are capable of now.
- See others lovingly and they will see you the same way.
- Your chosen sex helps you fulfill your life plan.

- Go higher in your thinking. *Why are they experiencing those circumstances in their life?*
- Love one another. Repeat.
- Balance the intellect and soul energies.

Chapter 13

Pay Back Time

While you are on Earth meeting people, creating, playing, exploring, and enjoying all it has to offer, you also spend a portion of this lifetime correcting any unkind actions toward others and being careful not to repeat old mistakes or make any new ones. Your choices and actions affect everyone around you. To pay back a debt to another is to bring balance to your soul. You are polishing and perfecting all the lifetime lessons. You created this life experience and are joyous to have the opportunity to return to others what is due them.

Everyone around you is doing the same thing. If another has harmed you, in time, this injustice will be made up to you. Maybe not in this lifetime, but someday. The responsibility of the misuse is given back to the offender. When you are harmed as you have harmed another, you then know and understand not to repeat the misuse. In this respect for life, you honor those who are a part of you by not taking or wanting their things, talking badly about them, blocking their energy flow, or wishing them ill will.

Did you cheat or lie? Were you irresponsible, silent, or angry? Did you take advantage of another or stop another's freewill in the name of God? Did you judge others, set in motion negative thoughts, hold back too much, help too little, deprive the spiritual seeking, or fail to see yourself in another? These are the actions and reactions and the stuff that creates debt. And the right use of it in abundance creates a bank full of good energy.

Now remember, the last paragraph isn't just about this lifetime now, while you are reading this book. It involves the soul experiences needed to correct wrongs of all of your lives. Just think, there are souls who get down to their last lifetime on Earth. What an adventure to do it one more time to see if you have the lessons down pat!

Sometimes, people feel that "something" is not right. They must "do something." They are out of the flow and the soul energy is pulling them back with this thought. When you refuse to use your own energy flow, when you fight it because you don't like what you have to do, you can build massive amounts of karma. One builds karma when they blame others.

There are situations where debt is not incurred, such as the actions of small children, the mentally deficient, Alzheimer patients, those with Down syndrome, the autistic, and soldiers in war with service at heart without malicious intent.

Sometimes it takes a long time, if you are counting, to have all the right people and circumstances in place to perfect your soul. It depends on what you need to learn or fix, and whom you owe. If a soul has gone Home and has earned the right to stay Home, you may repay a debt to another who is due the energy.

Do you know someone who has it all—abundance in all things? Do they live well? Do beauty and good people surround them? Well, there is a reason. It is due them! Perhaps they lived one or more lives of deprivation, hunger, and need. Perhaps they did so in a way to exalt their soul and learned very hard lessons. Now they are experiencing what is due them. How will they grow and treat their fellow man in bountiful circumstances? Then again, the beggar on the street may have been a greedy person who refused to share, hoarded his wealth, and treated others badly. Now he experiences the opposite to know what it is like. This may be his best way to repay misuse.

You may have already experienced the whiplash of your own bad choice and have paid for it. You won't do that again. Maybe you repeated a story about someone, later found out it wasn't true, went to them, and apologized. You righted a wrong. You may have been envious of your friend's achievement, so you ignored them, belittled them, or hurt their feelings. Later, your conscience bothered you when you got an award, and you wanted everyone to pat you on the back. Learning from your mistake, you made up for your selfishness and praised your friend.

The teacher, Jesus, taught forgiveness. He chose to do so in an extreme way, so the lesson would be remembered. Forgiveness is one of the most difficult wrongs to right. You don't have to be the unforgiven one to experience forgiveness. Jesus went to the trouble of putting himself in this position so all could learn from it. He said, "Forgive them for they know not what they do." In other words, they are where they are in their understanding.

The people you know who seem to go with the flow, and who are able to accept their fellow man without a negative reaction or judgment, are rich ones in soul evolvement indeed. They have learned and remember this important lesson. They are expressing it through being a good example. How do they do that? We need to pay attention.

The following is one such example.

David is eight. He adores his Uncle John. They have a special bond from a previous life as soldiers together. This is not in their conscious awareness, but just *is*. They feel "something" good and strong between them. They love being together. David's mom, Sandra, is Uncle John's sister. Sandra has never understood John. He annoys her. She tends to speak negatively of her brother in front of David. Sandra and John have a debt to repay one another. That is why they chose to be siblings—to get the job done. No matter what Sandra says about her brother, her son, David, loves him and wants to do things with his uncle. His perception of John's soul energy and his mother's perception of John's soul energy are different because of different experiences together. This is why everyone doesn't like, love, and feel the same way about everyone. Different stuff is going on in individual soul growth. No matter how old you are, something on that blackboard can be erased and rewritten with a new thought. Awesome!

When one says, "Wait a minute. Let me rethink this," or "Give me time to digest this," or "Maybe there is another way to look at this," they have picked up the eraser.

You may know of drug addicted or alcoholic parents who shared their energy and created a child. As awful as you may think it is, they have the right. The soul who comes to them knows who they are, and has chosen a difficult situation and path to live. Maybe this child will follow in their footsteps. Maybe it will be their salvation. Maybe it will grow to teach, love, and care for them. There are many choices along the way.

The personality in the material world gets carried away. People can hurt others terribly for what is thought to be their gain. For a while, it may be their gain, but not forever. One should get away from these souls and their negative use of energy and wish them the best on their path.

People who intentionally kill others and who are dangerous indeed need to be removed from society. But you should not kill them in kind for what they have done. They will pay in time for taking another off their path, but it may not be in your time. No one has the right to take another's life and take them out of their life plan.

People on Earth have horrible, vicious things done to them. Their bodies are violated, their freedoms are taken away, or they have loved ones taken from them (kidnapped or murdered). Their property, their hope, their best is taken and beaten and disregarded. Their dreams and visions are thwarted. They are disliked, judged, and ill-used by their own kind. There is a lot to forgive to be able to go forward. One can become a slave to not forgiving others or one's self. The energy of such a person doesn't flow. It drags, like being bogged down in the mud. Slavery of the spirit (holding on to old thoughts) is self-imposed. All slavery is not physical or imposed by others. It takes work to release another in love, and forgive them, even if you tell yourself over and over, "What if it were me?" Deep pain and betrayals break the heart and scar the soul. The memory can be deep from life to life. Until you clear the weeds, you can't begin to plant your garden. Begin to make the effort, little by little. One day, someday, you won't even have the unforgiving thought anymore and it will be DONE!

Perhaps, in a past experience, you were critical of a race group. Maybe you were awful, nasty, or cruel and taught others to be so as well. You misused energy by not recognizing the best in your fellow man no matter his or her race. Often, the best way to fix this misuse is to place yourself in a body and situation like the one you judged, so you come to understand deeply what that experience is like.

Perhaps if you were a slave owner, you may now become the slave. If you were bigoted, others may now be bigoted against you. If you were extremely judgmental of a body type, mental ability, or belief system, and you could not expand your thinking to recognize the perfection in your fellow man, then whatever you railed against, now becomes your experience. You set up with others the circumstances that will help you grow. That is, you selected your own little school within the big Earth-school.

Wow! If mankind could just keep this in mind every day, he would think before he spoke or took action. He would know without a doubt, that any misuse he creates he must "un-create" and repay in like kind someday, somewhere, somehow. It is a divine law. It is what we all decided.

There are fellow souls galore to help you. Many have been there and know where you are in this. Just try, my Dear One, to begin. You also know people who get in a rut and refuse to change their energy, or couldn't move when the energy changed around them. They often look to others to get them out of the rut or to give them contentment and happiness. Or they run from person to person to help them. When you have done your best by them, release them. Perhaps they need to learn from another person.

Children pick up their new flow of energy easily. They will struggle against the parents that try to stop them. Some young souls will allow another to stop their growth. A wise parent or friend will say, "Do it yourself. Make it right."

Some souls chose to experience a great deal of trials early in life. Maybe they are sickly, or in poverty. Maybe they don't have the basic needs. This can be a way of paying back debts. The same may be true of a soul in physical old age who lingers to allow others to care for him. The caregivers have a livelihood, and are loving their fellow man in this stage of life and may be making repayment in this line of service. You just never know. Amazing, huh?

People go in and out of one another's lives. If you owe a life long debt (or it will take that long), then you will be with this person. Consider fifty-year marriages, twins, and lifelong friends. Everyone has witnessed a relationship where the one person is horrible to the other, and he or she just keeps on taking it. This could be "getting what is due them." They didn't leave when the writing was on the wall, and now have trouble doing so. You never know.

A lot of people have said, "What does he see in her?" You

don't know and may never. Something is going on for sure! Others could be saying this about a relationship you are in! A man or woman may have lined up two or three souls they owe from a past relationship bond. One by one, they may choose to pay back in a marriage to these souls to fulfill their plan. Not every marriage is meant to go on and on just as not everyone was designed to be a parent. When the lesson is done, the energy is finished and released. It is time to move on.

Often, people stay on after a debt is paid. One knows if you are to continue with the person involved or to remove yourself completely. What can happen if you are meant to go but stay past the time you set up? New karma can be built to deal with this. An example would be: from some past life, a woman owes, in repayment, the joy of children to her husband in this life. It is their agreement to satisfy. The agreement is also to then part ways, as he is to spend time with another mate and she is to go forward with her plans. Maybe she is to become a shoe designer. Who knows? Anyway, they set out a plan and what they would fulfill to a certain time and then go on separately. Well, this is their business and a good soul growth righting. So, what if all goes according to plan? They marry, have the children, and it is now time for her to go and she doesn't? Uh oh! The script of the couple is altered, as are the lives of the people they were to be involved with and that of their children.

Well, this is okay, as all choice is okay. One or both may be fighting the energy because of social influences that say, "Divorce is wrong. How can you leave your children? What kind of mother are you? How will *he* manage the kids? You are a terrible example. This doesn't happen in our family, neighborhood, town, faith. . . ."

The higher self of the soul KNOWS. It will keep you on your plan when the personality is strong. Divorce and change are extremely difficult. It isn't easy for the core people involved—

Mom, Dad, and kids. It is deeply painful at the time, but they know the energy is finished and it is time to move on. The script calls for a change of plans. Or it could be a gradual change that flows because the higher selves have an awareness that it is okay. If one stays too long, the relationship can become hateful, negative, and destructive because the souls are holding themselves back from the courses of their lives. Then everybody is building karma left and right, and not enjoying life. The people who made all the judgmental statements build karma, as do the ones who chose not to follow the original plan. And not only are those who stayed in the situation hurt, but so are those you never met because your plan with them was not fulfilled. When you are aware of this, it can make you crazy. No telling what might have been!

Other examples may be children who need to leave home early and are biting at the bit to go experience life away from their family. Parents want to stop them, to protect them. However, you must remember, my dear fellow soul, that each situation and choice is unique, as unique as each soul involved, and each molecule of air, and drop of ocean water. In choices, two plus two does not equal four. I, your Angel, can't say, nor can you, that . . .

1. She put out his eyes, so now works with the blind or experiences blindness herself.
2. He was a nasty jailer, so now tries to improve the penal system.
3. He hated her, so they choose to learn love through being twins.
4. She expressed great love, so now enjoys abundance and being loved.
5. He cheated his employees, so now is the employee learning fairness with a difficult boss.

6.   She lied about intentions of love, so now doubts others' feelings.

7.   He was bigoted to gays and blacks, so now he feels others' prejudices.

8.   Her mother hated her, so she may now have a difficult relationship with her child.

9.   She was homeless and deprived, so may now live a protective life with all that's needed.

10. He beat his wife, so may become an abused person to understand the negative power of violence.

It is not this simple. This could be the reason for some experiences, but the thing is, you just don't know and it's none of your business! You must remember that if you were a person who hurt others, you yourself will choose a situation to learn the right way to make up for any harm. It may not be as clear as the examples above. There are thousands of variables in relationships and lifetimes. Just one correction could be experienced, or perhaps fifty. It is up to you. Keep in mind that every soul, no matter how good or evil, is a part of the All and expressing their lifetime according to their soul's needs and plans. One can't know what quest another's soul has chosen in which to grow.

The soul can go seemingly backwards from a great contributor to mankind to a very simple existence. The reason and choices belong to the soul. Don't confuse the outward appearance, personality, or collection of personal goods with soul growth. A person working with just the bare necessities might be the most evolved soul you know.

You all have the right to every idea and means of creation you desire. So, what recompense (righting of wrong) you devise with whoever, is solely and uniquely yours. Therefore, the Alzheimer, cancer, paralyzed, deaf, primitive, odd, common, simple, unusual, elephantiasis stricken, sickly, leprosy, over-sexed, lazy, holy, dictator, crazy, beautiful, comatose, nasty, manic-depressive, cross-dresser, homeless . . . are about the life plan they wrote for their experience to learn and perfect their soul.

If you are in their life, there is a reason. What is it? Think about it. Then remember, this is a good thing, as wrongs are corrected, if that is the case and you are a part of the opportunity to fix it. Ask yourself, "What is going on here?"

A woman may not want to be a mother. Maybe she has been a mother over and over and over again, did it well, and now this lifetime, she chooses not to bring children to Earth. A person may be unattractive in a family of beautiful people. Maybe they need to know what this is like, as perhaps they made another feel like an ugly duckling. One may be murdered. As awful as it may seem, perhaps somewhere in time, they were responsible for taking someone out of their life path, so they may now be forced to leave early through another's choice.

When you are born on the planet Earth, you are not alone. You are a part of a family, a community, a country, and a galaxy. Everything you have ever thought, said, and done has affected these groups. Not only can individual souls incur karmic debt, but groups can build karmic debt as well. When energies are combined and misused, causing others to be hurt, damaged, or knocked off their paths, then group karma is incurred. In time, the group must work together to repay this debt.

You could be part of a karmic group at work or in your neighborhood, family, political, or religious group. Several friends could be reunited to work out a past debt. Often, siblings are learning together and repaying a debt. Your child once could now be your parent or the parent now the child. It depends on what is needed and agreed upon. Very often, one parent may not be close to one child, but the other parent is. The mother could have agreed to bring the children to the father for the relationships they need to work on. Or the father agrees to be in this parent role and all the interaction and lessons are between the mother and the children.

This often explains why some children may say or think: "I didn't really know my father." Or, "My Mom and I never got along." Another thinks, "Dad and I are so close, but I don't have the same feelings about Mom." Or that, "Dad favors my sister. We just don't hit it off." Still another might say, "I'm the black sheep. I don't have anything in common with my brothers and sisters." Or, "I'm the odd one out in the family." Others will question, "Who are these people I was born to?"

Well, you chose them and their place in life and on Earth. And you also chose the other people with whom you wanted to learn. Comfort yourself. Think about it. It is okay that you don't love or aren't loved by everyone in the same way. No one is. Try and think lovingly about the parent with whom you have less in common. You probably don't have any karma with them. This is a good thing! So don't build any. Their main relationship to work out could be with the other parent or siblings. Count your blessings—one less hurdle. Not every member of every group is a key figure. Some could have just chosen the situation to experience.

Maybe you were a factory owner and took advantage of your employees for your profit. Perhaps to learn that this is wrong to do to fellow souls, you put yourself in the employee position to know first hand how it feels to be cheated and misused. Or you are part of a work group that in the past (maybe as a family) didn't live well together. You could hate your job, yet stay, and don't know why. Maybe you are not yet finished learning a lesson there. Can you figure out what you need to learn? When you do and it is done, you will move on to another experience. Maybe another group you need to understand, study with, and play with. Once the lesson is learned, it is done. When your karma is repaid, you have freed up energy to go forward in changes. It is why relationships change and people move on. You better your soul, love, knowledge, and understanding and life becomes smoother, as you've graduated, so to speak. You would not go back to grade school or high school. You did it. It's done. But this doesn't mean you know everything. Life is ongoing learning and soul perfecting, with chance after chance to graduate. No one yells at you, pressures you, or puts you down in your soul advancement. It is privately and personally your timing and your choice.

One may choose a service-to-their-fellow-man role—a president, senator, or mayor. These life choices take on a huge responsibility of leadership. The soul urge to do so may be in order to right the wrongs inflicted on a group, whole state, or country. Whole countries can have a karmic experience to live and work through. Poor Poland has been so brave. In wars, this was the country everyone had to march across to get the other guy. They chose to serve the world with an example of faith and fortitude.

It is not just all about you! It couldn't be when you are a part of the All and inseparable from the All. Even the bad guys, the devil energy, the mean and hateful, are a part of the All. They just have buried themselves in deep repetition and karmic debt. If you know them, maybe you chose to be with them to guide and help them! If you have tried to help and they refuse your energy, then move on and do not get caught up in it. Since these negative souls are a part of you, you have the obligation to help. But, if the student won't learn, release them to another who may be able to help.

Remember now, all beings created this merry-go-round. The personality of man is a playground of emotions that often can get one into trouble. The rule we set up is: You are free to do anything but hurt one another. If you do, then you fix it!

This is what every soul on Earth is about—glowing, growing, loving, creating, fixing adventuring, and playing. Even when you are finished here and go Home, you still make choices and go on and on. There is much to do, see, think about, and be. And you can't help but create. You are creative energy. Nothing ends. It just changes—and not until you make it change.

Aren't you incredible? And so are the rest of your fellow men and women. What fun everyone should be having on his or her mission/vacation on Earth. If it isn't fun, then you must be an intense worker, under another's thumb, or of limited thinking or education. If it is anything less than what you can think of as an "enjoyable life," then you have put yourself in this situation to grow. Bless you for being about balancing the universal energies for everyone and yourself. When you see and know people in difficult circumstances, know they are bravely fixing what is due, or due them. Send them, in thought, some love to help them on their way. Yes, all men and women are equal. Everyone is a part of the same energy. But by our own freewill, we forgot the best use of our energies and in universal agreement, promised to remember and right them.

On the Earth, there are the poor in spirit, money, needs, and health. There are those who struggle for these things and there are those that have just what they need and those that have more. There are also those who seem to have too much in abundance and spirit. Every single one of them chose the circumstances from which to experience and learn.

REMEMBER . . .

- Go with your own energy flow.
- Recognize others in theirs.

- You are responsible, as a student and teacher.
- You can change what is on the blackboard any time.
- Your life impacts ALL life.
- You charted your own path to live.
- There are no set rules on how and when misuse must be repaid—just that it must.
- Souls choose infinite and colorful ways to express their energy.
- There are two body models on the Earth with millions of variations.
- Everything is energy.
- Focus on your goal here.
- Planet Earth is a smorgasbord of souls from every where!
- Know when to move on to grow.

Chapter 14

Love Relationships

Keep in mind the big picture. All previous pages have described it and explained it. I'm so proud, as is the Universe and your guardian Angel, of your open mind and heart, to hear some new ideas. Entertain them and talk about them to loved ones. You think you are alone sometimes. Confusion, distrust, and lack of personal companionship sometimes hurt you. You are a Universe within yourself and since you recognize how magnificent you are, you want to share it with another, intimately. A lifetime is difficult to walk alone, if it was not part of your plan.

You could have set up a great plan and been very detailed, like writing your life story, and filming it. You said, "Okay, I will be male and have black skin and be born in the South of the U.S.A. I will have parents who teach me discipline and siblings to whom I can repay debts. I will get an education, and date three gals I need to touch base with until the love of my life comes into mine. We will marry and have a family. I have agreed to bring four children—three good soul mates I wish to share with again, and one child to whom I owe a great deal, and will repay the karma."

Well, so far so good. Everyone does this. They write a script and choose a vehicle (body), circumstances, and other soul groups. But it is written with chalk, and others have a right to alter plans, just as you do. The parents you wanted may not be available. They may be having trouble fulfilling their path. You may not meet your spouse. You may have two, not three children. Another person, misusing their energy, could harm you in a drunk driving accident and alter your script! But, just as you have vacation plans, you have a plan B, in case it rains and you can't go to the beach. The soul bounces. It is resilient and tenacious. I have "vacationed" before on Earth. It knows the big picture, the whole story, though sometimes it needs reminding and gentle loving to go to plan C, D, E, and on, if necessary. So the last words you may hear from Home before you are born, may be: "Be flexible. Things can change!"

The soul desires to shine and share. The soul is love. When one is IN LOVE, they have tapped into the perfect energy of the All. It is exhilarating and glorious. One may say, "I've never felt this way before." But you have. The earthly matter and distractions kept you so busy. Living on Earth in a body calls for moving a lot of things around every day: food, dishes, clothes, cars, thoughts, more things, and emotions.

To just BE, and remember the Home energy, is difficult to do. But when two people meet and click, they remember one another, like recalling a dream you had last night. You say, "Oh, yeah. I remember now." They chose to blend their energies and love one another. They are recognizing the energy of Home and their origin. They think and feel new life, resurrection, a lifting up, and the surge of pure energy through their mind, body, and soul.

When babies have just arrived from the All, we are drawn to their glow and perfection, as they come with love. The elderly and dying who are going to go Home have a glimpse and reminder of the love there and the thrill of completion. Their souls are sparkling to be welcomed lovingly back Home.

What about this person you can't get enough of? The one you hanker to get closer and closer to? The one who makes you feel special, wonderful, handsome, and smart? The one you want to be your best for? And why, after time passes, do you

NEVER forget the first days of love and its lightening zap to your mind and heart?

You don't forget awakening love because it suspends your soul in a Home or All energy that is perfect and not contaminated, dented, or misused. With some, when the person they loved is out of their life plan or goes Home, they search for the sensational love energy again. It is such a heady, fun, safe, soft, comfortable feeling that others strive for, talk about, write about, sing about, and celebrate.

Are you another's reminder of the energy of Home? Or is another's yours? After love is lost, some can hold the memory without expressing it again in physical form with another. For some, once may be enough. For others, ten times may not be enough. It depends on your soul need and story.

Some fellow men and women are in complete service to everyone. They use their earthly years in helping and praying, such as monks, nuns, etc. This is where their soul growth is. Jesus, Buddha, and Gandhi are examples. Some may not choose a mate and family. They desire to learn the lessons of standing alone. They, too, are lovable and loved. They can be good examples for many. Perhaps all their debts are paid and their twin flame is Home. All is complete with them; marriage is not a necessary energy state for them during this lifetime.

Think now of the differences in feelings you have for people in different categories. There are people you feel obligated to, perhaps, such as your parents, the boss, the sick or poor, or a group to which you belong. There are people you have fun with and whose company you enjoy such as your grandchildren, a neighbor, a parent, a friend, or a co-worker. Then, there may be the person you love, admire, respect, wish to be like or think you are like, and with whom you wish to share your life. You wouldn't want to live without them.

Karmic Relationships

In a love relationship, when you feel an obligation, it is usually a pairing you set up. This person can be a spouse, child, sibling, or friend. It is one who you knew before in a lifetime and shared much. You planned to be together, so you could repay debts to one another. If you choose to be spouses, then you commit on a higher level to work things out. It may be a lifetime together to fulfill the karma or for a brief time. An example. In the past, a father and daughter were at odds because he wouldn't release her to marry her true love. He cheated her of her future and the lessons she was to learn. He was selfish. This lifetime, they agreed to share a life and now he is the husband and she is his wife. He owes her love, compassion, and the things she was denied. So, he is a generous husband. The karma may not be lifelong, by their agreement at Home, and she may need to leave him to go on with her life. Hopefully once the karmic debt is repaid, in time, they can release one another, debt paid. She gave him the opportunity to do this by returning to the Earth-school with him.

You may feel an obligation to your wife or husband. It is not an easy, flowing relationship, because a lot of work is being done. You have a job to do with one another. A mission, some resolve, and support. Most often, you won't know what it was until long past. But, just as you knew when you met them, you must do something with them, you will also know when it is finished, as much as you know to close the book after you have read the last page. That's all there is! This time is a time to rejoice. Whenever you give another what they need, you are filling their soul with love.

Soul Mates

You can have many karmic and soul mate relationships to fulfill your plan. There is the karmic mate just discussed, and the soul mate relationship. In these two, you can have many and go from one to another fulfilling your plans. Soul mates also have shared past lives with you and agreed to do it again! Only you are not indebted to one another. The love, the length, and the lessons are all set up in agreement to help one another grow in soul development. They usually are truly good friends and consult, blend, live, and laugh well together. It is a "pretty" energy to be around couples who are soul mates. They help the other think, rejoice, stretch, and soar. This is often a fun relationship, very flowing, and both serve and teach the other.

What couples can you think of that share this type of marriage relationship? Most people have a best friend that this describes. You just "click" with one another and enjoy being in each other's lives. There are soul mate marriages that blend the male/female energies. However, two males or two females can be soul mates. These are souls who have experienced past lives together and agreed to help encourage one another again.

Twin Flames

Then, there are twin flames. Your twin flame is the one other person who is your balance, your help, and your other half. Your core energy is one and the same. This person is soul familiar, which is more familiar than "intimate." One feels that his heart cannot beat, nor could the Universe contain the passion, melding, and completeness without the twin flame. Whether you are with them or not, you know they are somewhere. You both are about your own individual soul's experiences. One may be older in soul experiences than the other. Or your souls may have experienced equal growth. They are your home at Home when you are there at the same time. You could be here at the Earth-school, and your twin could be home, learning and waiting for you, protecting you, helping you. Or you could be marriage partners on Earth. Strangely though, the twin-flame marriage is not the easiest.

Now, how did this come about, you say? Often, the term "soul mate" is confused with "twin flame." The soul is light-like energy, hence the word "flame." And "twin," since at one time, way, way back, you were both one flame and one energy—a part of the vast and endless All. Then one day, "part" of you decided to break off. This part is just as whole and complete as before the parting. Remember, the flame or soul has all creative energies and freewill. One half may say, for example, "You know, I'd really like to zap out to that planet Pluto and see what it is all about." Well, the other half may have no desire to do this at all, and says, "Okay, you do that and you can tell me all about it. Share your experiences with me when we get back together." Meanwhile, the half flame that stayed home may get the urge to travel. Perhaps it has heard a lot of discussion from souls going to and from Earth and wishes to go to Earth to study and understand what "time" is. This soul that is always in contact with its twin, and lets the other know of its plan. The Pluto traveler may say, "Oh, okay. Have a great time. Be careful. I'll see you in a little while, and we'll share experiences." Sixty, eighty, a hundred years on Earth is a small time in all of eternity. This is all done in thoughts, of course. In this example, one half is on Pluto, and the other half goes to Earth. They are always aware of one another. When a soul comes to Earth, it chooses a sex, as these are the forms used to express and experience on the Earth. Usually, when both twin flames are on Earth at the same time, one is male and the other female. It's a balance. However, there are no hard and fast rules. There are gay couples that are twin flames, where both chose male or female bodies. It is not the best situation and can be difficult, but the reason there aren't many rules is because the divine expression of the Universe is "Love One Another." If you follow this, you are not going to hurt others. Remember, you can't judge. You do not know what another's plan is or what they are working on.

A five-year-old could be a twin flame to an eighty-year-old. Twin flames could be continents apart and never meet, or a relative in your family. They can share great passion or a love-hate relationship. It depends on what they set up to learn from this experience.

How often do people say, "Well, they deserve one another!" Well, this could really be true. They may have hard lessons to learn through all sorts of situations.

It is difficult to describe how unlimited energy is and what you can do, have done, and will do with no limitations. Your energy is contained in a physical body. Limitlessness is hard to grasp. Most souls choose to split and have a twin flame because it is more fun and enhances each one's gaining of under-standing. When twin flames rendezvous at home again, they share the understanding they gained in experiences. In under-standing, there is soul growth. You are one and the same, yet individuals. However, one's soul growth is not the other's. One could devote his life to feeding the hungry and gain vast soul growth doing so. You can share this knowledge with your twin, but he or she would gain in soul growth in the same way only by experiencing this himself. Just as, if your twin is an ax murderer, you wouldn't want the karma that came with that!

Buddha and Jesus both said, "What I can do, you can do." And this is so. You just need to believe it and do it! Not all souls split their energy. But most do. Jesus, Buddha, and some other high spiritual leaders do not have twin flames by their choice. This decision was made eons ago, before their lifetimes from which you know them. They and others are very evolved souls who put themselves in service. They did not split their energy because it was all needed to be who they were to teach in service and accomplish what they came to do. They experienced many lifetimes to gain soul growth and also had many soul connections with love and support to help them, just as you do. Their focus was to be in human body form on Earth and to be known as Buddha and Jesus. These lifetimes were their pinnacle of service to All. You must remember that their energy is constantly pulled on at all times. It is their mission and their joy. For them, it is living their dream.

REMEMBER . . .

- Having the opportunities to fix things is wonderful.
- The feeling of love is remembrance of Home.
- Not everyone planned to have a mate.
- Karmic relationship—Buddies go on a trip together to apologize, make up for, and fix past hurts due one another.
- Soul mate relationship—Buddies go on a trip together to be one another's fan club, support, teacher, and to offer encouragement.
- Twin-flame relationship—One who makes you whole. The same energy sharing through eternity and beyond.
- The best plans can be altered by other's choices.
- The lifetimes of Buddha, Jesus, and the other teachers are still a constant joy for them.

Chapter 15

Love, Sex, and Forgiveness

The blending of thoughts, ideas, values, and creativity between two people is fabulous. Communication and sharing, once a connection is made, is the foundation of any relationship. Moving forward in shared dreams and goals sustains it. The emotions are triggered and warmth, desire, happiness, liking, and loving are expressed through the words and actions. Then, sex, the blending and sharing of two energies, is the physical expression of love. Or it can be just an exchange of energy if love is not involved. In either situation, great care must be taken for right use of this exchange, since it is the very blend of great creative powers that makes life anew. This is by our design. We created the male and female physical forms to be in service to all other souls to make bodies for them to experience through. Just as your parents gave you the opportunity, you may, this lifetime, give it to another. As with thoughts and words, responsibilities for one's actions are always the bottom line!

If you do not care about your fellow men and women, you can be hurtful, deceitful, selfish, destructive, cheating, and careless. This can occur through thoughts, words, and actions. Sex is a powerful action with extreme consequences for selfish misuse. It can be a sacred act of sharing between people deeply committed to one another's well being. It can be like a friendly handshake among friends, or it can be a base act of gratification because the opportunity was there. In any case, responsibility must be accepted for sex and the results. After all, it is, on Earth, the action that results in the creation of a body for a soul to choose to enter for its evolvement and growth. As with every action, a person must think: By this action, am I harming another? Am I harming myself? What could be the consequences of this action? Am I prepared to pay the debt it may create either now or later in another life? Would I want someone to do this to me?

Sex is great. It feels good. It is supposed to. It is natural. It's fun. Just remember, if you misuse it and harm another through this act, you will know and experience the seriousness of misuse.

Everyone carries different energies. One may put their energies toward music, engineering, art, or fishing. Some people dedicate themselves to medicine, the law, or religion. They set up energies in this life to go about these goals and energy uses. And some people, for their own reasons and needs, set up a lot of their lifetime energy for sexual use. Just as one doesn't know why, but knows there is a reason. A person may be a monk or politician, a prisoner, slave, accountant, or an actor. One can't judge why another would spend a great deal of energy on using sex as an everyday expression. What is the prostitute doing? What is he or she learning? There is something going on. There always is with every single person on Earth! Everyone is about his or her business, whether you think it's right, wrong, great, crazy, odd, awkward, sick, funny, strange, or weird. The slimeball pond scum is experiencing. What do you need to learn from the type of person they are?

Often, it is hard to see another as a part of us because our emotions come into play. We think quickly, "I can't stand her." Or "He's stupid." Or "He's foreign and funny looking!" So what! They are they, you are you, and you both are one. Your entire life on Earth will become instantly easier when you can let go of judgments of others and replace your judgments with new ideas on your blackboard.

New ways to think about situations: "How interesting. She comes from another culture." Or, "I wonder what she is learning from choosing black, white, red, brown, yellow skin?" About a mixed marriage (of race, religion, or both): "My—how brave they are. I wonder what they are working on?" Of a gay couple, "They are gay! I may not like it or understand it, but my fellow men and women have a right to their choices and expressions, just as I do."

Why would one choose to be gay in this society that has so little understanding of it? Why do people put the Bible and other holy writings that emphasize not judging, up between themselves and the gay person, to proclaim them as a lesser person than themselves? Why does a soul choose anything different from what is considered "normal" to any society into which they are born? All these choices are made because they need some experience to live and energy to express to perfect their soul.

Can you think, "What if it were I? What if it were my child or grandchild? How will my soul accept, love, and respond to them? What is going on?" If this is very hard for you, try and get a grip on it. Do not judge, unless you wish this experience for yourself. After all, if one of your loved ones is gay, you agreed at Home, before you came to Earth, in the script you wrote, to bring this child, this soul, as one with whom to share a lifetime and from whom to learn.

Sex can be an expression of great passion and comfort, a casual act, or a horrible violence. There can be joyous sex or a sick violation. Sex is an intimate exchange of energy and profoundly affects a mental picture of one's self worth. It can bring you to the heights of contentment or the depths of evil. It is the stuff of curiosity, gossip, fear (rape), plot, power, playfulness, and a lesser-evolved soul's misuse.

Western societies warn their young about sex's addictive

powers tied tightly to emotional choices. Yet, some of these adults do not handle their own emotions or sexual choices intelligently. Once again, some examples are best not followed.

Loving sex is meant to be an awakening of the evolved, physical body form, a passage from function to fun. It is a time to share and play and be special, a time to blend energies and create children, if this is chosen. Mankind has laws and expectations of men and women for order and their protection. As with all energy expression, there is responsibility, therefore, with whom and how is no one's business but those involved.

Forgiveness

Forgiveness is tough. It's like your belly is full of ball bearings. One by one, you've got to get them up and out and away from you, or nothing can flow through your belly again. Not forgiving clogs everything and affects those around you, especially if you can't forgive yourself. Being unforgiving comes out of you in anger, bitterness, and judgment. Often, you blame others. To forgive can be a long process. Begin by repeating who and why. See the pain coming out of your pores like sweat. Get it out. It's poison. It makes you sour and sick.

Remember, you are not perfect. You have fellow souls to help you. Resolve it in this lifetime if you can. If you can't, you will have another chance, in time. Give those who haven't forgiven you the opportunity they need to make it up. If they can't, know that in time, they will.

Remembering the teacher, Jesus, helps. He was betrayed and abandoned by all his good buddies, but one. They were afraid. He was viciously murdered and very misunderstood. His mission was to teach love and forgiveness. Often, it helps to say, "If the big guy can do it, so can I!" You are a part of him. Only good and freedom can come of it. Begin as soon as you can. Your Angel is on your side. Call on him or her for energy and wisdom to help. You have all the time you need.

Not everyone likes or hates the same people. Their life experiences, past and present, draw you or repel you from energies that remind you of your own lessons. We connect with others through what we like or don't like about ourselves. You may have worked eight lifetimes to learn to be humble. So, a braggart would grate on your nerves. We admire those who have achieved, as we have an appreciation for the time and effort it takes to grow. You have a right to your opinion about everything.

When you feel, "They betrayed me. Stabbed me in the back. Damaged my reputation. Gossiped about me. Spread rumors. Made no effort to understand. Pushed me away." You may ask yourself, "How do I forgive and go on?" Try to train yourself. The minute you hear negatives about anyone, say, "Stop, is this truth? Who is this person speaking? Why are they saying these things?" Sometimes it is innocent talk. Other times, it is malicious cruelty meant to damage and to make the gossiper seem knowledgeable and important. Be a smart soul. Immediately put yourself in the victim's place. Say something like, "Do you think it wise to talk about this?" Or "I don't need to know this." You might even say, "Would you like another person discussing you?" This is a hard situation, as most all conversation is about your fellow men and women and how they behave and lead their lives. It is like breathing. But pain and harm to another's sense of who they are, whether the truth or not, is misuse.

A dear one has been ripped from their life path in progress and caused unspeakable, unbearable pain to those who lost him. This soul will have to begin again. Many life paths were altered. The experience of loss of life in any matter is deeply sad. It hurts. A violent death at another's hands is unimaginable, because all are from the same energy. The soul at fault, will, in time, know every aspect of the pain and fear of their victim. It is better that they be removed from society and lose their freedoms and choices, in order to think about their actions, and prepare to go home by natural death, as they must return in time to repent in another life and repay the soul interrupted and their loved ones. Some call this state "hell." There is always justice. We all just can't see it. You never have the right to take another's life. This is the one "never" in the Universe.

Take time to think about what you believe. You may be unhappy because you don't understand another's actions. It may help you to forgive yourself and others if you think on these ideas and suggestions. . . .

Wow, there are hundreds of different religions! I wonder which ones I've been involved in during past lives? Why does the one I belong to now help me? And those who don't go to church, I bless them on their way. It's okay.

The homeless, the hungry, the uneducated, the physically, mentally, emotionally challenged, the ugly, the beautiful, the poorest, the richest—these are my fellow men and women. All are a part of me. They each have a story and a challenge. I think of them and treat them lovingly, as I could be one of them!

What are violent, angry, depressed, shy, wild people experiencing and why? I need to think about them more closely. Usually, lack of love has damaged them. I send them love and protection. Thoughts are real things.

Abortion is wrong! This thought feels right. But how do I know what is going on with this woman and this fetus and their life plan? I will send loving thoughts to them both. I will do the best I can in my own life.

A good thing to say every morning when you get up is, "May only truth pass my lips." You have brought forth the highest and reminded yourself that you are spirit first.

What kind of people do you like to talk to and be around? Who feeds your needs and shares your ideas? Who are you comfortable with? We would only choose to be with nasty, cruel, destructive people if we needed to be exposed to them to learn or teach. We keep trying and trying with some people, because we recognize the need in others to learn and find their way. Often, we have been there and want to help, since we know the struggle, know we can help, and know that that's why we are here—to help. But we have to quit when, after honestly trying, another won't, can't, or refuses to use our energy. Perhaps there is another who can help. Or, they need to figure it out on their own. Release them to their own good.

REMEMBER . . .

- Sex is an exchange of energy.
- All energy exchanges come with responsibilities.
- Think before you speak, act, and judge.
- A good thing to say every morning, when you get up is, "May only truth pass my lips." You have brought forth the highest and reminded yourself that you are spirit first.
- Isn't the human race on Earth interesting?
- See how they run.
- See how they solve karma.
- See how they speak and act.
- See how I am one of them.
- Thank God/All, that I have all the time I need.

Chapter 16

Rock of Ages?

What shall this time be called that I am writing in now, and that you are reading? Will the 2000s be referred to as the New Age, the Age of Aquarius, the New Millennium, the Information Age, the Age of Ages, the Age of the Universe, or perhaps the Rock of Ages? Men and women need to label time. This is good—it keeps everything in order. Every day we are constantly arranging things—energy, emotions, ideas, and material goods—to create order.

Hopefully, most people have learned or are learning, that the material things on Earth are fun, neat, and all evolved from a single idea. You are on Earth to create and play with the stuff on it, because you had the single idea to do so. Just as the filthy rich person flies to Paris in their own jet for lunch because they can, you are on the Earth, because you can.

If your life lessons are in kindergarten, that is where you do your studies. If it's grade school, high school, college, or advanced studies, that is where you may choose to experience growth.

A human soul does not go back to lesser evolvement. When you are done on Earth, lay your body down and go Home, you do not have full knowledge of the Universe and all under-standing. If that were so, we would not all be in this cycle of study, learning, and experiencing, lifetime after lifetime. There would be no need. One progresses each lifetime perfecting lessons and rounding out one's soul growth.

Your energy just can't sit home in the All very long without creating. Change is what energy does best. Energy is in constant flow. Picture the planet Earth in the line-up with the sun, other planets, moons, and stars. This is your galaxy in space. You can't see all of it, like you can't see thoughts, but it is there—a universal flow of energy of which everyone is a part and to which everyone has access. Picture a strong wind that is lit up and weaves in and out and around the sun, moons, and planets. This universal energy flow picks up all the thoughts, ideas, and happenings everywhere. When you are looking for a new idea, or a different way to go, picture yourself reaching up into the universal flow and drawing out of it what you need.

Very often, people will come up with similar themes for books and movies. You see them repeated with different variations. Someone, somewhere, had the idea, and it went out on the ethers in the universal flow. Someone else picked it up! If you don't want your ideas copied, just say, "I block this for another's use now." You have the right.

At times, some people will pick up information before others do. They may put it in print, on television, or in movies for everyone to see, enjoy, or think about. Some souls who have done this and nudged people's thinking along have been: Orson Welles, *War of the Worlds*; Rod Serling, *The Twilight Zone*; Gene Rodenberry, *Star Trek*; George Lucas, *Star Wars*; and Steven Spielberg, *Close Encounters of the Third Kind*. No doubt, it is a part of their life plan, to teach and serve their fellow man in entertaining ways to enlightenment. They may not even be aware of this. There are many others in all areas on Earth who have contributed to the soul advancement of mankind—in politics, the arts and sciences, and in literature.

What they all present are new ideas and new ways of thinking. Often, it begins in a small group, such as with Buddha, Mohammed, Gandhi, and Jesus, and spreads out by word of mouth. With satellites, the internet, fiber optics, and television, you now know five seconds after a queen has blown her nose! This leaves the big barn door of responsibility wide open, influencing billions of people, not just a small group. Imagine a karmic debt on the misuse of a harmful and negative idea of this magnitude! Not a pretty thought.

What if the five creators mentioned earlier (and there are many more) were to get you used to the idea of space travel? You would get used to odd-looking beings, plus fantastic inventions for everyday use in healing and living. Some people cannot imagine these things ever, and these helpers might be able to educate you and excite you, preparing you for the next two thousand years. Chances are, you will return to live in many of them. Little by little, ideas are forming about one world, one planet, and no boundaries. This will take eons to come to pass. But think of how many destructive thoughts have to be rearranged and deleted, century after century, to make it an acceptable, let alone, workable idea. In the 1900s, it was horrible to see a woman's ankles! Time, mass thought, and fashion changed that. It used to be cool to smoke cigarettes. More time and mass thought changed that. In another fifty years, it may be a serious taboo, or even illegal.

Religions of the world are being given more thought. The more educated man becomes, the more accepting and kind he becomes. Someone sat down and listed all the religions of the planet, and figured out that all of them focus on one source. Everyone agrees that they want to be treated well. It dawns on them that, to receive this treatment, they must treat others well. Religious faiths are becoming more recognizing of the oneness of man. Not only one certain belief group will go to Heaven! How could that be?

Many, many rules, dogmas, and guidelines were established as religious law for people to use as moral and spiritual boundaries. They were necessary, and are necessary for souls striving in their script with these needs. Whatever works for one's own soul growth is good. After all, the bottom line or purpose of religion is to remind you that you are soul first. All souls are in a state of becoming and are doing fine at their pace. Even for the nastiest soul ever, there is hope. Others can teach, advise and show you the way, but you must do the work, as you, alone, are responsible for your soul growth. You are your own judge and jury, and will set up for yourself the next lessons to help you grow.

You think life on Earth is real. It is a great creation, full of amazement and variety in all things. Reality is Home, which is vast, better, and free with a oneness great in joy and perpetual ecstasy. This is where you begin, and because you can, and you choose to, you venture forth as you wish.

In different times on Earth and in man's history, teachers have come forth to present new ideas through the examples of their lives. Earlier, Confucius, Buddha, Jesus, Moses, and Mohammed were discussed. These past two thousand years have been dominated by their teachings through a multitude of interpretations. These lessons were so important and rang so true that lifetime after lifetime, attention and care came back in thought with souls to carry those truths forward. Each teacher taught according to the mental capabilities and education of their fellow men and women of the day. Jesus' day would be considered primitive compared to today. Life was pretty basic. The world was small. The population was a small dent in today's numbers. It is amazing that Jesus' message, as well as that of other teachers, has been repeated and repeated, used as life guides all these years.

Mankind has definitely grown from just a physical body surviving, to a being taking mental leaps and learning awesome skills. Sometimes, a person remembers one's source, other times, not. Soul evolution takes time, no matter the setting, whether it is Nazareth, Cairo, Beijing, Rome, Istanbul, or Los Angeles. In all man's creations, you knew you were more than flesh and blood, bone and muscle. You may have needed reminding each time you lived, so you built mosques, temples, cathedrals, chapels, and shrines. Fellow souls have dedicated their lives to reminding others who they are.

Some pretty scary ideas were taught, too, such as a vengeful God, hell, sin, and damnation. Also people have said, "Believe and live the way I do or I will hurt you, kill you." The salvation got all mixed up in the survival of the group. Others urged, "Let's go on a crusade, take other people's stuff, convert them, and haul them back Home, whether they want to go or not!" The planetary energies have come a long way since these days. Some areas of the world are still isolated in their ways and beliefs. It may be a long time until they can change ideas and think of themselves in oneness with the Universe.

There has been a constant idea, repeated and reinforced, that men and women only have one life and one chance. "You only go around once!" This is very limiting in a limitless Universe. How could this be, when energy, which we all are, cannot be destroyed and is always creating? Who has made love or had sex once and not wanted to do it again? Who has heard their name spoken and been told they are loved and not wanted to hear it again? Who has taken an exciting trip, met great new people, and has not wanted to do it again? Who has heard a beautiful song and not wanted to hear it over and over? Who has enjoyed a good laugh and the thrill of some surprise and not wanted to experience it again? Who doesn't get up each day and think, hope, and work toward making something good happen? Look for the resolve to feel better and do better, and to do so day after day.

The sun rises and the sun sets. Earth rotates and revolves in its solar system. This system is just one in the

All/universe/infinite energy. We create, un-create, and re-create, as do animals, plants, and all living things. It is a small thought to believe, "This one life is it." Though, for many, it is a safe thought! The rules say, do this and that and you're done. What a surprise to these souls, when they return Home to be so absolutely free, and realize that they are bigger, better, and infinitely more special than they ever imagined. What a relief to then learn that, no, you won't be going to purgatory or hell forever. Rest a while. Think a while. When you are ready, plan your next trip and take it. Then come back Home, as we love you. By the way, every positive use of the energy of which you are a part, benefits everyone for all of time! Wow!

For some, it is difficult to be responsible for their own soul growth. A ruler, leader, God, father figure, is necessary, in some minds, to protect and punish. They need someone to blame when things don't go the way they want. You often hear these phrases spoken: "God has a plan. Why did God do this to me? I am mad at God. How could God let this happen? What kind of God would let children suffer and catastrophes happen?"

In each of these statements, replace God with yourself: "I have a plan. Why did I do this to myself? I am mad at myself. How could I let this happen? What kind of person would let children suffer?" Do this because you are God, part of the All, and you are responsible for your own soul growth.

The "religion" for this age could be called "Humanity." Every soul would recognize the good in themselves and their fellow men and women, through honoring and serving one another. And guess what? Every time the awareness of oneness dawns on a mind for the first time, there is a second coming of Christ. The messiah has arrived. Christ, the enlightened one, is you! The Messiah, the messenger is you! Fireworks go off in Heaven. Every soul before you rejoices. You get a standing ovation. Your soul is born again in a new, positive, wonderful truth. Your soul has jumped the river, climbed the mountain, swam the ocean, lifted the burden, and turned on a floodlight of new possibilities. And you can't back up! Now, every person you see, talk to, and know exists, is connected and one with you. You are very aware of it. You have nothing more for which to wait and no one else for whom to wait. The Universe is at your service, and the rules are easy. Examples are everywhere. Now you are a teacher and example.

The great teachers spread these truths, as do modern day teachers, with understanding, compassion, love, and goodness. They walk and work among you. They can be someone well known to everyone, or someone down the street, quietly expressing unconditional love.

You are wonderful. You have rights. No matter your place in life, a teacher sees you and recognizes the good in you. You are a part of him or her. Each soul strives, whether in the dirt, or in a castle. How can we help one another?

One of our modern day teachers was Princess Diana. Now, don't slam this book shut! Remember, it is not always clear what another soul is doing and how or why. Judge not. Despite what you have heard and read about Diana Spencer, you did not know her script, or her goal and purpose on Earth. You have not walked in her shoes. In contrast to the other teachers discussed in this book so far, she serves as the example that was not obvious. She seems too flawed to be listed in such wise and contributing company. Oh, Diana was very flawed. She chose a difficult and brief life path, and crammed in a lot. She then left, tragically, so that you would remember her, think about the good in her, and copy it in your life. This was a soul who had physical imbalances, not enough love, was lonely and misunderstood, judged, scrutinized, and watched daily! Remember that she, Charles, and their sons set up this script.

Maybe the mother she chose was to leave her to impact on her the type of mother she needed to be. Perhaps there was karma to work out between, Charles, Camilla and her. Who knows? In the past, Diana could have been the "other woman" and damaged another marriage. This experience was of like pain, to know this kind of betrayal. To live it on a stage, before the whole world, must have served some monstrous debt to erase. One can't know. But because all of these people are a part of us, we owe them some second thoughts. We should try and benefit from their examples.

A group karma involved the entire royal family. Remember, you keep returning with the same souls, if you need to work things out with them. The history of the British Monarchy is full of wild behavior, vengeful actions, and power plays. They all have not yet been worked out, so maybe this is why this monarchy still exists. Like Big Foot, the vehicle is still needed to serve the energy.

Diana was able, in all her problems and shortcomings, to hold in her mind every day that she was a part of every soul on Earth. She reached out, smiled, and touched them. If for only two seconds, her love lifted another. She spread ocean waves of love through her looks, touch, and kindness. This is called the Christ Consciousness or an enlightened one's consciousness. Her wealth, position, notoriety, and the sensationalism surrounding her provided her platform. They made her life more difficult but gave her a more visible position from which to serve as an example and to touch many lives.

Jesus' stage was a small world. However, the truth he taught was so strong, it has endured in the minds of genera-tions since his day. He was different, so more noticed. His family thought him strange. Diana's stage was the whole planet. She reinforced the same truths. Being a woman and royalty made people notice, and her family thought she was strange!

They walked among the people everywhere. They talked to them and touched them. A smile, kindness, and touch are powerful energies. Both of them could look at all people and love the highest good in them. They made each person they met feel good and special. Both were humble souls. Both held on to the energy without a mate to support them. They knew their strength came from the All and everyone they touched!

The countries in Europe and Asia are so old and so strong in traditions that their thoughts don't allow many new thoughts to enter. Change there is slower to take hold because of this group consciousness. Diana was a light in her corner of the world, to awaken many to their own beauty and possibilities.

By now, you may be comfortable with some new thoughts as to who you are. You are probably putting a lot of thought into who your parents, children, friends, or spouse is. This is good. The more you know, the better you use positive energy. Now, every time you greet a brand new baby, you can look at it and say, "Welcome, Little One. Who are you? What is your mission? Am I a part of your life plan?" Be overwhelmed that this soul has made a long journey. You have a head start, so help it all you can.

You are also observing choices people have made, and what their lives are like. Some say, "I must live right. My life is good." They probably have lived "right," and they are basking in what is due them. Others are moaning and groaning. They need some inspiration. Can you give them some? Can you really want for everyone else, what you want for yourself? Can you praise your neighbors? The more people who feel good, the better you will feel. This feeling ripples onto the whole world. See what power you have?

Your soul is the power company, generating the mental, thinking you. It is positive and creative. Your emotions and feelings activate your personality. The emotions can be destructive, but they help with balance. Your physical body is affected by what you think, how you feel, and how you react. Illness is often caused when the emotions get carried away. The personality takes hold and won't let the mental get a thought in edgewise! The emotions can get carried away when one thought is stuck in gear. Since thoughts are real things, these energies have to go somewhere. They can't go up, to the mental, so they go down into the body. For example, nasty, toxic thoughts may create a tumor. Being stopped, held back, kept under pressure, or restrained can lead to arthritis, a crippling of the joints that limits your movement. Worry, stress, and insecurity can create an ulcer. Fear can paralyze you and cause heart problems. Not being able to speak honestly can lead to TMJ or lockjaw.

The body reacts to what the mind has thought. Think about some of these things, if they affect you. Is there a reason that your body is in pain? Your fellow men and women are healers of all sorts. Seek them out and let them do their service to help you flow in comfort. Have you chosen this pain to learn something or teach another?

You have "come a long way, baby" in reading this book. Good for you. Maybe you can use some of it. Speaking for your Angel, as you visualize him or her, I want you to:

1.   Become a creative power on Earth, for your own good, as well as others.
2.   Love your true self and the personality you chose to work with this life.
3.   Be aware that the personality sees flaws, but the soul doesn't!
4.   Accept your life path. Embrace it. You wrote it.
5.   Work every day to transform what is negative into the positive.

6. Remember that creative forces are at work in each man, woman, and child.

7. Greet everyone you meet with the best of yourself. Be conscious of their best. These thoughts will bring it forth.

In your culture, you say, "Hello, how are you?" It happens so quickly. It is not a greeting really heard or responded to, as it can be. Taken to its best energy, everyone could be thinking and saying, "Hello, soul on Earth, made of energy like me. I greet the beauty and best in you. I honor the path you have chosen to perfect your soul and repay debts. I, too, am doing the same thing. Can we help one another to grow and serve our fellow man?"

Oh my, just think how different some conversations would be, if men and women recognized themselves in one another and beheld all others as holy, special, and unique. From the gal behind the counter at the gas station or tollbooth, to the professor and executive, to the child getting started and elderly person wrapping up their life. From one energy you were all created and to one energy you all return.

REMEMBER . . .

- You live in the now, no matter what you call it.

- You are because you can.

- The Universal Flow is the "yellow pages" of all existence. Reach up and get what you need.

- Some souls serve by giving us new ideas and pictures to get used to.

- Even the stinkers on Earth want to be comfortable.

- There is only one religion, which goes by many names. Each soul interprets it for his or her own growth.

- "Please keep moving. . . . There's no stopping the energy flow."

- Sex is great. It feels good and makes more people. Maybe one is your teacher!

- You are the Messiah who has come again with the idea of oneness! Wow.

- Teachers come in all sizes and disguises, all around the world. Pay attention.

- Say, "Hello, fellow soul. What are you doing here? What is your itinerary? How long are you staying?"

- Erase the junk from your blackboard. Write on it:

  Health, Love, Wealth, Wisdom, A clear and big picture, Love for everyone, Love for self.

Chapter 17
Balancing

Why did you pick this book up and choose to read it? For fun or conversation? We hope for both. We, your beloved Angels, ever present with you on your path, wish you to explore all possibilities.

The Earth planet is heavy. So are your bodies. Wonderful and exciting things have been created recently. You have heard, now and then, of a kid that can pass advanced college courses at eleven or twelve years of age. But when he closes the books, his emotions and body are still eleven or twelve. The child that he or she is comes first. The emotional and physical areas have to develop in stages through experiences. They don't get to drive a car or fit in with adults.

Some places and in some societies on the planet, the intellect has soared with the vast possibilities the computer creates. Here, too, as with all tools, there is room for misuse. No sooner had a system been designed to alphabetize a list you entered in the computer, than someone entered pornography that could be alphabetized. Everyone wants to search and know. But you have to be careful what you do with what you know.

In a short time on Earth, life and its comforts for its creatures have exploded. You can get a car with heated seats or a rack to heat your towels! Food can be prepared quickly. You can make a phone call from an airplane or a mountaintop. You can send images around the world in seconds. In 1860 and 1960, these would have been considered magical. Repairing broken and malfunctioning bodies is an art form. The knowledge of the human body space suit is well understood. What a scalpel once did, a laser does now. New and improved energy uses have been discovered.

Finally, touch and love are being given their due as powerful, anesthetic, or healing, helping drugs. There is, at last, more understanding of mental and emotional illnesses. There are no longer state institutions to hide and care for these long suffering souls. People have learned that there are reasons why one is manic-depressive, paranoid, dangerous, hyper, or afraid. Man's intellect has figured out what pills, herbs, or treatments can help these distressed souls.

Cancer, AIDS, muscular dystrophy, cystic fibrosis, sickle cell anemia, Alzheimer's, diabetes, and other illnesses challenge the soul's body and keep busy those who came to explore and study how to change and rid the body of disease. Balancing the mental, emotional, physical, and spiritual is a daily challenge. All are in and a part of the Spiritual Package Deal!

The danger lies in allowing the mental, emotional, or physical to rule the life path! It is like trying to drive to Denver on a direct highway, yet you keep taking detours. To get where you are going, you have to retrace steps to get back on the main road again. You can't allow the road signs to lure you off in other directions. A mental detour could be playing games with others and yourself or when you keep thinking over and over again the same thoughts in the same ways and having the same results. It is like watching a movie repeatedly. It will end the same way every time, unless you or someone else thinks of and films a new ending, and makes it available. How do you want your story to go? Do you want to travel from Tennessee to Denver through Chicago, Minneapolis, and Cheyenne? It will take longer, but it's your option to go any way you want.

The emotions do what the mental tells them. This is the playground of the personality. It can express great character, or baby pettiness! One can get lost here, playing a long time. Often because it is easy, and one doesn't want to pick up their emotional toys and carry them home to put them in order. Usually, there is another who is happy to play with you and keep you here.

The physical goes along with the emotions and the mental. The physical ends up carrying the load. It can't pick up the toys, a physical activity, until the mental tells the emotional that it is time to go in and stop messing around. Then, think about how we will play differently tomorrow. It's like the old joke of the doctor asking, "What hurts?" The patient says: "It hurts when I bend my elbow!" The doctor says: "Don't bend your elbow!" The physical body is going to hurt some way, if the mental and emotional get worn out, stressed out, shut out, or found out. The emotions will cry and be depressed, sad, worried, forlorn, and miserable when the mental can't or won't change the idea that creates the distress. Everyone, every day, thousands of times, changes negative energy to positive energy.

Here are some examples of turning a mental negative into a positive. Try turning the thought "I dread another day at work" into "Thank God I have a job." Or "Those kids drive me crazy" into "How lucky I am to have healthy children." If you're first thought is, "Oh no, it's raining," remember, "It's good for my garden." Don't constantly complain, "The car is old" when you can be grateful that the car runs. With any negative thought, try to think, "I can get through this, I can handle this." Or ask yourself, "Is there something positive about this experience?"

Of course, there are situations created that no amount of the mental can alter. This would be of the soul's choice to experience and live through, for themselves or others. It may be karmic that your body is paralyzed, has a deformity, or ends up in a vegetative state. For these, the emotional hurdle for balance is acceptance. Being. You need to find out about your situation and think about it to change it. This isn't done in a noisy room, in front of a television or computer.

Be still, and know that You are God. You chose your life path. Be still and pray, meditate, or think in a positive way—however you connect with your higher self, and allow your spirit self to guide you. Ask for guidance and help. Ask for wisdom. Ask for the big picture. Ask for the map to get back on the highway and off the bumpy side roads. Ask for a helper, teacher, or mentor. Blend the spirit you in your thoughts. Blend the spirit you in your emotions. Blend the spirit you in your body and actions.

Sometimes you look at people's difficult situations and think: How can they take much more? Their energy is not your energy. They have profound lessons to learn or teach, and may have chosen very difficult tasks. Bless their path. Are you involved in some way? If so, help. If not, go your way and learn from their positive or negative energy example.

Often, illnesses are karmic. The person chooses to go through physical, mental, or emotional discomfort, to know what it is all about and understand. Perhaps they did not show compassion and patience to another before, with the same illness. Or this experience is their best way to repay others. They could also be serving to give those who care for them employment, and time to learn from their body. You just don't know for sure.

Have you ever felt guilty when you see people with very little, doing so much for others? How about that person who rescues every stray animal, protects them, and finds them homes? Or people who have many children—their own, adopted, some with handicaps, and problems, too. Or there's the person who volunteers unselfishly throughout life or raises money (energy) for worthy causes. There is no need to feel guilty. This is what they came to do with children or animals or organizations. You may have done the same in a past life or will in another. They could be building dharma in this life mission. For sure, they are teachers through example.

1. Some people are the thinkers and organizers: Let's help children.
2. Some people are the doers: Provide a home, love, a lap, nurturing, and fun.
3. Some people are the helpers: We'll sell raffle tickets to help the doers, do the "service."
4. Some people are the receivers: If it hadn't been for Joe and Sally, I wouldn't have had a home.

It is fellow men and women together, creating a flow of good and love. Are you one of them? Or are you a lone person leading a simple life, just taking good care of yourself? This choice could be a monumental task. It depends on what your soul needs to do and why.

Mankind gets in trouble when his intellect gets too big for his mental britches! He tends to forget his source. He forgets that he is one with others. He can get a big head and become self important and controlling.

REMEMBER . . .

- Blend your Spiritual you with the Mental, Emotional, Physical you.

- Keep your map out, so you can find your way. Stop and ask, if you can't read the map. You can't read a map in the dark.

- Accept karmic choices.

- Praise other people's life plans. Action. Comedy. Tragedy. Romance. Black and white. Technicolor. 3D. Silent film.

- Learn from everyone.

Chapter 18

Universal Thinking

Group Consciousness

We have had shifts in consciousness through the ages. At Home, as well as on the Earth-school, everything is open to discussion. Though we Angels and souls here are thought energy and do not have bodies, we recognize one another by the vibration or sparkle of our energy. On Earth, you look different. Your voices sound different. You are different in sex, color, size, and also have different energy vibrations. Just like you on Earth, we here, do not always agree on everything. Your planet school is very ancient and has been heated, watered, frozen, cracked, jarred, erupted, and windblown! The masses of land have been arranged and rearranged. The Earth is a living mass of soils, rocks, water, and minerals. We all created its wonders over eons, eons, and eons of time. It is a lot to conceive, let alone believe. But it's true. It is a masterpiece of a planet and regarded as such in the galaxies.

The planet, like its inhabitants, is in a state of becoming. Constant change is going on. In the later 1900s, you recognized that so many on Earth were mistreating the environment and have worked diligently to preserve its waters, forests, and air. Great care has been taken to protect and preserve all the creatures that live there. Stewardship of land and ocean harvests to nurture living matter was accepted and studied for all Earth-kind.

These are all positive moves to counteract the abuse the Earth has taken. Deep holes have been dug in it. It's been bombed. The oceans have been used for dumping. Landmasses have been rearranged to make way for roads, tunnels, and tracks. Millions of miles of concrete have been poured on it and green forest areas cut away. Lands and water are contaminated with oils, poisons, and toxins. It may not have been you personally, but a mindset that you are a part of, which took advantage of the planet's bounty. This is group consciousness. A group may think, at one time, that an idea is okay, like slavery in the United States when buying and selling people was accepted as okay. This way of thinking is horrible. It took a lot of suffering, sacrifice, and changing of a mindset for whole groups to know and believe that everyone has the right to respect and freedom. There are yet places on Earth where many are slaves and this lesson has not yet been learned. People say, "It wasn't me or my family or group or religion that was cruel, hateful, or caused this or that to happen. It was my ancestors and they have nothing to do with me now." When you believe this is your only life and opportunity, this belief is understood. However, you and everyone else are responsible. You were in the past generations. You were a part of group decisions that affected the paths of individuals and civilizations. You are at this time, too.

Armageddon, Apocalypse and the Rapture

The idea of an "end" is in so many people's group consciousness. It has been a repeated thought through lifetime after lifetime. Just as we all prepared men and women in the days of the Roman Empire and Jerusalem that a Messiah would come by repeating and repeating this message. He did come. He lived, breathed, laughed, and loved everyone. He accepted the task of loving—to be the messenger of love. His audience was small in comparison to all the souls on Earth now. Confucius, Buddha, and the others paved the way for him. Jesus, the man and teacher who knew absolutely that he was part of all of us, went against the thoughts and beliefs of his day, one person against a group consciousness, to make a dramatic statement to turn a way of thinking in another direction.

Jesus did it! His followers and disciples repeated his words and example to inspire everyone to do better for their soul growth. Here we are, two thousand years later (because we need to count), with the right idea and his lesson of "Love One Another" intact. It is also expressed in all other faiths and religions in their own ways, all over the world. Remember that "Christ" means "Enlightened One." You do not have to be labeled Christian, Jewish, Amish, Muslim, Hindu, Buddhist, Mormon, etc., to know that without loving one another, not much will advance forward! If reference to the messenger, Jesus, turns you off, replace his name with a title or name that you follow and admire.

The example of the United States abolishing slavery did not change the attitudes the group consciousness had about the black race. Only after generation upon generation of changing language, negative ideas, and attitudes, will this group consciousness be altered.

Along through time came the positive teachings of how to treat one another. Along with it came the idea of an end—Armageddon, an Apocalypse, or Rapture. This was part of some interpretations of teachings. It was built-in motivation to be good, to follow the rules. "If you are bad, you will go to hell." All men and women kind will suffer horribly in the end. It didn't matter if you were saintly or not. Everyone would be judged in a lump. Doom would befall everyone. Fire, flood, and disease will destroy civilization. Lots of punishment. An anti-Christ ruler. Some repeated the idea that the "chosen" ones would be saved and the bad would be left on Earth, a post-end hell, to fend for themselves! Rapture. These messages of doom have never been "deleted," since they could work so well to motivate an ornery soul who is hell-bent on creating havoc.

To think, believe, and search for self and soul purpose, outside of a man-interpreted religion, one must brave being different and have absolute trust in the God or All. You would have an instinctive memory of the law that all energy is good and that you have freewill. This idea has prevailed in the shadows before recorded history. There is nothing new here. It is the way it is. It just may be new to you now. If this is so, then this is your time to chew on it and think about it.

One is just as "safe" or "right" within the walls of the different religious rituals, as one is in their own rituals, in practicing love and goodness to all. You need not be damned by thoughts of a catastrophic end. A terminally ill person may be motivated to put her life in order, given the advantage of knowing when her physical life on Earth will end. Or, the idea of the body dying limits the freedom of possibilities that could yet be and perhaps even changed, if this is the plan. To wait for an Armageddon, Apocalypse, or Messiah is to deem yourself terminally ill. It limits you. To think life, love, and time is never ending, always changing, forgiving, and boundless allows your soul to soar, laugh, glow, dance, sing, and be, for yourself and towards all others. Jesus and Buddha did not teach damnation and suffering. They taught forgiveness and love.

Armageddon is the name of a battlefield near Megiddo, a city in Syria, southwest of Nazareth. It was predicted that here would happen a great battle between good and evil, and then God would reign supreme. Let me tell you, loved one, that Armageddon is an old race thought that goes back many thousands of years. The body of knowledge of the world and the philosophy of life was quite small. It is part of the human condition that gives one joy to believe that even those who are successful will "get theirs" one day. Armageddon is an awesome word! And word of mouth has never let the idea die out. Just remember, there is no end. Certainly, since we are all a part of one another, we do not wish ill will upon others, our enemy or ourselves. Besides, you and your enemy will redo what is necessary and right all wrongs in time. Remember?

There is another word that strikes fear into the hearts of believers. Apocalypse. This, too, is an old race consciousness thought. This one, however, was planted and repeated by those who looked to the darkness. Do not allow fear to be a part of your daily thinking. You are in control of every step you take and choice you make. No one else. You are not going to go blind from masturbating, meet your end in plagues, earthquakes, pestilence, and famine, or be hauled off by a horse rider named Death. Don't even entertain the thought. Make room in your storeroom of knowledge for more interesting, loving, and positive thoughts.

Another very limiting belief is of the Rapture. Rapture is another great word. It sounds and feels so glorious and complete. Unfortunately, it is a strange and limiting idea. However, those who have faith in it, do for a reason. Somehow, it is a guideline for them. It is where they are in understanding. It is the belief that, at the Second Coming, only believers will be carried away by the power of God. This belief has caused much anguish and pain. How can it be that so few would be better or chosen above another? We are all one. Again, the human condition to feel superior plays into this belief. The truth is, every soul will be rapturously complete in the God or All energy in their right time!

Isn't it more glorious and easier to live daily, believing in endless possibility? Think of things just five years ago that weren't available or thought of. Think of who you were five years ago, and how you are different now. Think of how your politics, finances, romance, or knowledge of technology is different. Think how brave you are every day to go to work, be among the masses, get in a vehicle, and decide to do or not do this or that. Think of how you open your heart to love and hope. You have so much now at your fingertips to explore. Information galore. There is no need to be in the dark. But, you have to turn on the light so you can see your way, and you must recognize that every living being is in the same boat as you. Reach out for help and knowledge or be available to be the helper. Everyone has a mission. Teamwork gets the soul soaring!

Visionaries

Mankind just loves the idea that someone knows what will happen in the future. It is natural to be curious and it is fun to dream. Dreams are thoughts, and thoughts are real things, so stuff happens. But remember—by your choice! You can always change your mind, go another direction, and do as you please. It is your divine right of freewill. Yes, there are people who are visionaries, people who can "read" the possibilities in your energies. A loving and good "reader of your energies" will make it clear to you that no matter what they "see," the choice is always yours. Many of these souls who are open to this are in service to mankind. They are to be of loving guidance, often to direct you in a constructive way to go. Some weaker personalities can get caught up in the ego and the attention and the money involved for this help. Beware of those who would tell you negative news or speak ill, without understanding, of another or of a situation. No one has this right, as it can influence your choice and alter your path or that of another. These seers create karma, big time, for themselves. It is a tremendous responsibility to advise others through readings, tarot, palmistry, etc. These are all good tools, and exist for guidance, just as religions do. Use your own intuition to "feel" if the one you consult has the highest good in mind in their service.

A visionary who is looked at, quoted, and believed so often is Nostradamus. Nostradamus was truly a visionary and in touch with his God or All self. He was a mystic and beyond his time. His purpose in his predictive writings was to get the people of his day to look beyond what was right there in their everyday lives, to get them thinking differently and about other possibilities. Just as your Angel is in cahoots with me to tickle your thoughts and get you to think differently.

Nostradamus wrote, as Jesus spoke. He hid things in his writing, making them open for interpretation. He wasn't stupid. Jesus, in order to get a point across, spoke in parables or stories. They both addressed the mentality, education, and needs of their time. Nostradamus' writings were intended for looking forward at the possible choices of energy use for the next two hundred to three hundred years, not thousands. But man gets a thrill out of predictions. People keep repeating his forecasts or quatrains because generation after generation will pay money for the books about "What Will Happen Next?" He is a best seller! Many events have been accredited to Nostradamus. Some are not true. How could they be? Every person involved in every event had a choice. In those three hundred years of happenings, to be sure, many altered their paths and choices. Remember that man and womankind likes the idea of someone else in control and "in-the-know." If someone else is in control, then they are not responsible. Chew on this.

Shifting the Shift

When you choose to consult any of the tools at the end of this book for guidance (see the Important Lists and Lessons section), put out the thought (pray) that the server speaks the truth and is guided by their higher self and a consciousness of oneness. For yourself, ask to hear clearly and to use your new information lovingly for all concerned. When you need a situation to change or draw something new to you, you have to figure out how to do it.

Group consciousness over the last hundred years has been thinking about how to get all people to really look at one another, help one another, and learn to work together. The planet Earth was due for a cleansing from all the misuse and abuse. All souls born on the planet since World War II came with a soul knowledge of being part of a cataclysmic event involving the planet shifting slightly off its axis. This would cause enormous loss of life, the destruction of buildings, loss of utilities, and all the inconveniences experienced in great earthquakes and floods. Everyone would be affected. One country or rescue team could not go to another to help them. Everyone would be forced to see and help the one beside him or her. It is in man's nature not to respond unless there is an immediate need. A time of survival would follow a time of rebuilding and reawakening to everyone's spiritual self. It would be a long time before material goods or distracting technology would get in the way of people helping people and appreciating one another, much like the survivors of wars clinging together for support in a common memory of shocking change and loss. From this knowledge of things to come, the herbal arts, all healing arts and spiritual strengthening to serve one's fellow men and women, would be revived and restudied, knowing that hospitals and doctors wouldn't be available.

In the 1960s, the idea of communities working together simply and spiritually came forth in young people too early to be accepted or used. Eastern ideas were brought west. It was this group's right to choose and to try to influence society. Their ideas of "free-love" and "peace, not war," and use of natural foods and remedies were their gifts of a new way to be and act. They had to be different just as groups before them. They had the right idea, and a lot of heart to persist. Society was not ready for the "flower-children" and their ideas. It was too soon. Some groups broke up and others slowly altered their ways quietly, and pursued the ancient arts, the tools that can enhance man's spirit and guide him.

Many souls also viewed this time as an opportunity to go to the Earth-school and have a short life, since the shifting would take them home. There was a window of opportunity to repay karma and work on soul growth. Especially since, after the shift, there would be less people to have children to provide a body for the Earth-school experiences. The population exploded!

Two other planets became unavailable for learning experiences and eager souls chose Earth. There is no holding creativity back! These souls meshed themselves into the best circumstances for them, and brought with them energy uses of different kinds—new blood, so to speak. A "been there, done that" group. The entire planet has become the melting pot of the galaxy! The numbers have grown. Never before have so many souls been on the Earth together. It is very exciting.

Meanwhile, another group consciousness was working out the question: "How can we achieve brotherhood among all men and women without a total destruction and rebuilding? Can it be done gradually?" They worked to find an alternative plan that would avert or hold off the shift, a Plan B.

As they were pouring thought energy into this, thousands of groups around the world were going about Plan A, studying together on how to survive, serve, and help everyone who stayed. Often, they are called unity or "New Age" groups. In a very short time, the term "New Age" scared people. It was not the mainstream thought. Some were looked upon as survivalists, which they were, but for everyone, not just their group.

They were people who were aware that a spiritual shift in men and women was due. They were preparing to provide all things needed, much like a ship's captain who knows his ship inside and out, and how to keep people safe in a catastrophe at sea. He has looked at all the needs and possibilities, and how best to go about handling a crisis. These groups made themselves available to serve their fellow men. However, since people are often lazy in their thinking, they make snap judgments. They slam the door on finding out what this or that group is about. Just as the "hippies" were deemed inappropriate and wrong, so, too, were these "New Age" groups. Then the cornerstone religions, not understanding what these groups were about and, often, not bothering to find out, labeled them as dangerous cults. Granted, some were led by personalities that misused their purpose and were destructive to individuals. Others were every day, hardworking, dedicated people who strive to practice their faith as do the Methodist, Presbyterian, or Scientologist.

The energy for Plan B was stronger and, eventually, was chosen. The expected Shift would not occur. When Plan A was phased out, the script for Plan B was infused with the energy needed for Earth souls to learn through gradual experiences, not one catastrophic event.

About now, you may be saying to yourself, "Who is in this group consciousness? I don't recall voting or being consulted." No, your physical mind does not recall your selection to be female and live in Texas, anymore than it does your part in a program to create circumstances affecting individual and group evolvement. But your soul does. You cannot be separated from the All. Even the negative energies of the "devil," the "brothers of darkness," and the "anti-Christ" are a part of the All energy.

The group is energy in thoughts. We all said, "Okay now, for us to get on with soul polishing and paying debts, how are we going to inspire the planet Earth?" One group said that a planetary shift would do it. After all, if everyone has to stay home, survive, and talk to one another, they will really see one another. It just may dawn on everyone about their oneness. Oh yeah, it will be a mess but the intelligence and technology is there. In generations, they will rebuild. But this time, because of what they went through, they will cherish one another and repeat and teach this lesson! Many agreed that this was a good idea, like people living in a war area saying, "Never again. It was too horrible. Let's not allow it to happen again."

Then another group said, "Do we have to go through such devastation and rebuilding? It will set the Earth back for centuries. It is looking good! Sure, some of our fellow men and women need a big blast of a reminder of who they are, as they are running amok off their paths and harming others. But, can't we have major lessons here and there that everyone will witness through technology? Let's give our loved ones a chance to respond and help."

Souls in favor of plan A and B began lives on Earth with their life plans all written for their missions. Many said, "This is great. I'll live, love, and experience what I've set up, then return Home when the shift occurs." Many said, "What an opportunity to serve, teach, and test what I know from all past lives. It's a chance to learn, a challenge to survive, then put the body down when I am done."

Everyone came equally dedicated to the part they would play. Some, in touch with their higher selves, remembered why they were here. They helped revive the use of herbs for medicines, survival skills, and techniques to calm and strengthen physically and spiritually. They thought of everything they might need to continue life and help all others, after the shift.

Many other souls had no clue, yet were a part of the plan. Some were the "flower children hippies" who introduced different language, casual living, and dependency on a small group for survival. Their ideas were of living simply, organic foods, knowing one's self, and sharing everyday responsibilities of tasks and childcare. Their parting words to family and friends were that they had to "find themselves!" As all groups that appear "different," the majority did not understand. Their mission was to present to the world another way of living, protesting, fighting, and dying in war. The hippies had children, and when the majority rejected this lifestyle, their ideas persisted quietly. The style and look of the groups blended in with everyone else. Meanwhile, old skills were practiced and tools for guidance explored, such as crystals.

In 1996, a shifting that would have caused much destruction did not occur as planned. The groups that were planning for this were made aware years before of the change, so new choices could be made for their life paths and others. Many who came with the intention of leaving for Home at the shift, have done so according to their script or as individuals. When mass energies change, scripts can be rewritten. Many had completed their lives and were ready to go Home. The souls that left Turkey for Home in the 1998 earthquake, were glad to be done with their physical bodies and hard lives. It was a group choice.

If it seems to the older-in-years souls on Earth that there are more storms, earthquakes, floods, volcanoes, hurricanes, tornadoes, and natural disasters, there are. This is a gradual way for one group to pitch in to help another group and rekindle in them a oneness, through disaster, that did not exist before. These awful things that happen bring out the best in people. They do not stop to think, "Is she in my club? Does he go to my school? Are they from that neighborhood?" before they reach out and pull them out of the flooding river! Nor should one ever, because you all do belong to one club: The Humanity Club from the All.

New Energies Enter

The Plan A group souls had to revise their scripts and sometimes, their commitments, jobs, and relationships. Some held to the course and some changed their course. Very gradually, people started using new words and having new ideas. They began doing things a little bit differently. It became popular to have your own herb garden or to be interested in organic foods and better nutrition for the body. Females continued stepping into jobs that had been predominantly male and males became more skilled at traditionally female jobs like child and home care. They experienced the balance. Acupuncture, medical doctors, and chiropractors began to blend their talents. Reflexology, touch, music, and aromatherapy were okay. In fact, if you had not tried it, what was wrong with you? Homemade things became valued. Satellite television showed us other ways to worship. Nations were trying to talk and understand one another. Mediating and negotiating became new ways of handling disputes. Groups everywhere for everything met to show compassion and support for divorce, gambling, drugs, diseases, deaths, crimes, victims, abuse, weight, smoking, etc. Religions opened new doors of thinking to "get real," so people could use their lessons. More churches and places of worship were built to serve and remind men and women of who they are. Some of the souls chose this era to be born in so they could advance technology. Where once the automobile, train, plane, sewing machine, electric light, telephone, and television were considered awesome, in the early 2000s, the population is adjusting weekly to rapid inventions of convenience. People will become used to having a phone in their pocket, a laptop computer, fax machines, touch lights, voice activated alarms, computers, CDs, digital sound, and a neighborhood movie theater able to download new films from satellite. Some will have experience with taking home movies or dealing with remote control gates, doors, toys, and televisions. You may have a car system that guides you to Grandma's and tells you when the car door is open or when the engine malfunctions. In the medical world, magnetic imaging (MRI) scans are more common, as are sonograms and non-invasive laser surgery. In other places of work, there are new things, too—from robots in factories to e-mail, e-banking, e-commerce, e-investing, e-nough!

And twenty years from now, these new and exciting things to work, play, and live with will seem as old-fashioned as an outhouse and icebox! Some ideas now seem old-fashioned! "Politically correct" is on everyone's lips. This is a conscious decision by groups to receive respect. When one says, "You will not slander and belittle this person," you are saying, "We are all a part of another and you must learn this. We respect you. You respect us!"

When a government calls another forward and says, "What are you doing here," the seed is planted that there are alternatives to violent domination. Even a "season of nonviolence" has gained popularity to honor Martin Luther King, Jr. and Gandhi.

More private schools and home schooling have emerged to fill a need for direction of discipline and curriculum. Standards and values are raised. People contribute more to charities and programs for medical cures. Please note, my loves, that as one energy idea stepped aside, another flowed in to replace it. Remember this. It is the same for your heart and soul and feelings. When one energy is exhausted, you put it away, let it go; another will arrive to fill the void. And once again, it is yours to do with as you please.

This is the Aquarian Age, the Information Age, the Light Age! Pick one. Light Age is good. Light food, light beer, light weight, lighthearted! Because you have the information, you can choose how to use it and see the Light! Granted, this description describes energies that are at a place in soul growth to use them. There are those young souls, remember, who have never seen a telephone nor need one. There is illiteracy, hunger, war, greed, need, and misuse everywhere yet on the planet. Souls of all evolvement and experience are sharing Earth together. What can you learn from one another? Russia, Northern Ireland, Israel, Austria, and China are examples. They have torn down walls, flung open doors, made room for new energy and new ideas. Brave steps. Scary times. Building a new group consciousness takes time. They have all the time they need. Send them loving thoughts. Thoughts are real things.

Interestingly enough, statistics screamed that Baby Boomers had not saved money for their retirement. They were spenders. They didn't plan on being here. The shift shifted, and so far, so good. The planet will eventually make its move to cleanse, but not for a while. Ideas shifted, too. Awareness of caring for the planet is strong. Its health is everyone's responsibility.

The other side of all the good uses in this awakening and information age is that the convenience of the computer can isolate men, women, and children. They have no farm to work to exercise their body as well as their brain. Now they must set aside time to go to the gym as well as to be with people and appreciate them. The computer cannot smell you, touch you, look you in the eye, see your expression, gauge your body language, hug you, hold your hand, and detect the beauty of your soul. It is a tool to enhance your life. Does it keep you from all of the above, or a good conversation sitting on the porch or at lunch? Can you sit it on your lap and tell it a story? Can you "spoon" with it in bed? Can you tickle it, feed it, wash it, whisper it your secrets? Of course, you can talk to other people and have a great time using the computer to communicate. But come the dark and come the dawn, it's nice to say to another, "Sweet dreams" and "Good morning!"

The purpose of technology is to bring people together through available knowledge and communication. It can. It does. But misused, as all things can be, it can have the opposite result and make strangers out of family members, neighbors, and friends. This information age might see young people bonding and marrying earlier to experience the need for compassion and completion. Be wise. Be balanced.

REMEMBER . . .

- Everyone is responsible for the planet.
- End of the world ideas have always existed.
- Armageddon—Apocalypse—Rapture—great words!
- Visionaries can see the possibilities.
- Plan A was "Let's start over (sort of)."
- Plan B was "Let's work with what we have."
- Are people taking care of people?
- Plan B, in effect. Weathering new storms.
- Out with the old and used. Delete, delete, enter!
- One is powerful energy. Group consciousness is awesome energy.
- The Age of Limitlessness.
- Love me, touch me, feel me, talk to me, hold me—and I'll do the same for you.

Chapter 19

Lessons

When lessons need to be lived and learned, groups and individuals set up events in order to do so. Unfortunately, planetary catastrophes and wars bring mankind closer together. They share a common goal of survival. Or an individual soul may need to understand patience or faith, and pour a lifetime of energy into situations that would teach this. An extremely impatient person may choose to become paralyzed in order to learn patience with those who care for them. Hate groups will certainly be the hated sometime around, so their souls will come to understand how ugly it is to take perfect energy and misuse it so destructively. Whatever you don't understand, you will study, live, and be. If you could recognize this sooner, rather than later, you could save yourself a lot of grief—and lifetimes. Everyone, however, goes along at his or her own pace.

Tolerance

As you read this, it is a time for tolerance on the planet Earth. It is a leap in Christ Consciousness to be tolerant of all people. One group that has set up lessons for you to consider, explore, and understand is that of gay men and lesbians. These souls, a part of you, are more visible and vocal. There are not any more homosexuals now, in accordance with the population, than in any other times. In years and ages past, homosexuals were quieter, as it was not worth burning at the stake to not be like others. Human sexuality tugs deeply at the psyche. Homosexuality frightens and repulses many. At this time on the planet, it is looked upon by most cultures with disdain. Some parts of the United States have taken the leap in Christ Consciousness to be tolerant of all fellow men and women.

Who do you think these souls are? Why are they here? What are they doing? Some have come forward this lifetime because they need to learn tolerance, or the lack of it, in other people's eyes. They could be here to teach tolerance. They may need deeply, once and for all, to learn to love themselves! Can you imagine the challenge of this alone? To be a gay man or lesbian is to be a very visible example to everyone. Their lifestyle challenges the best in people to think, pray, ask questions, become educated and elevate one's heart and soul in tolerance as we all want to be tolerated. We need to look at one another and accept the differences. Years ago, you may have had very different ideas about Germans, Japanese, Mexicans, Cubans, Blacks, or Native Americans. Possibly you had different opinions about smoking, drinking, drugs, fur coats, and what you eat. Years ago, a seat belt was hokey. Now, seat belts and airbags are the norm and helmets are next. Did you learn to like someone you couldn't stand or enjoy something you once didn't?

Things change. Energies change. What changed your thinking? You can do it again. Think on it, loved ones. You have nothing to lose and all to gain. It is tolerance to say and think "I wish this person well in their life choice and lesson. Help me to understand."

Remember that one of these men or women could have been your child. Think of their parents. The gays and lesbians did not hatch! They sprang from unions of love and years of nurturing, hopes, and plans. No loving parent ever wants their child to have no love for themselves, or to suffer from the meanness of others. Parents spend years and years just trying to keep their children safe and alive. When their child realizes that they do not think and feel like everyone else, the parents suffer heartbreak for their child's life and for their long struggle ahead in society. This makes the parents "different" also. Wouldn't it be wonderful if everyone realized that there is a much bigger picture? Then, so many would not judge, gossip, hate, and fear. Wow, think of the miles of blackboard ideas that have to be erased and rewritten to unconditionally love your child, or anyone's child, who has set up an enormous life lesson—not only for themselves, but also for the planet.

The teaching is to "love one another." Not to love one another with the exception of those who don't wear clothes like you, think like you, approve of you, don't use deodorant, have acne, have a bad hair day, are short, are ugly, smoke or drink, are homeless, are mean, dirty, sick, stupid, obese, speak another language, eat a different food, have a different belief, don't shave their arm pits, can't read, are blind, deaf, or para- lyzed, have slanted eyes, or express their love a different way.

Just, love one another. No exceptions. You say your religion is against homosexuality? What religion is this that would deny your fellow man his creative, karmic lessons or choices? You would not want to be denied your choice and experience. Do you think Buddha and the rest of the teachers would deny a person who is a part of them?

Acceptance is often very difficult, especially if the homo- sexual is your child or grandchild. You are God, they are God. The child chose to experience this lifestyle. If you can't reach some understanding or acceptance, can you be tolerant? Can you try? In being tolerant, can you not judge, speak, or act negatively to anyone about this choice? If you do, can you speak, teach, and be an example of tolerance?

You get to be who you are, in all your glory, no matter what you have chosen for yourself. If you would just try to allow yourself to look at and think about everyone you pass on the street, at the mall, in your neighborhood, at the airport, or in the sports stadiums, "No matter who and what this person is, they are about their soul growth mission on Earth, like me." You have heard the saying, "There but for the grace of God go I." When, for example, you see or meet another who is blind, this statement counts your blessings and all your lifetime efforts. It is tolerant and kind toward the blind person's life lessons.

Come Again?

When your heart, soul, and mind deeply and completely realize that you are one with the All, you cannot, in good consciousness, point fingers, blame, judge, hurt, destroy, or betray what is a part of you. The beauty of changing a negative energy into a positive energy is that it works like a great cleansing wave that starts far out to sea and rolls into the shore.

If changing an old way of thinking is at first difficult to do, then a surefire way to be tolerant is to really think hard to see yourself as that person. You know, "Walk a mile in their shoes." You are starting the wave with your thoughts and words. Once you start this and practice it, your heart will become lighter. The pressure of negativity will lift. It is like cleaning out a basement full of junk. You get all excited, because you have room for new stuff. And guess what? When you are awakened to the idea that you are spirit first and a part of your fellow men and women, and all souls everywhere, the Second Coming has arrived. The Messiah, the messenger has come. And it is you! You now hold the consciousness of Confucius, Buddha, Gandhi, Mohammed, Dalai Lama, Princess Diana, Moses, Mother Theresa, Martin Luther King, Jr., and Christ.

The beauty is, you will sparkle and practice treating

everyone with more tolerance and love. You will be an example to the next guy. You will be patient with those who aren't there yet. You will understand that, in their time, they will also arrive at this enlightened place. Wonderful, new energies will begin to flow to you—new ideas, people, opportunities, and blessings. You threw out the junk and made room for the new. You really are something else and are so loved by so, so many! Your Angel wishes you could see yourself as he/she does. You are never, ever alone on your trip to the Earth-school. Your Angel is like AAA, American Express, and your country's embassy, all at your service. If you don't ever ask for guidance, it won't come. Your Angel can't interfere with your choices.

Go look in a mirror, into your eyes, and say hello to your pure self. Say, "Dear Angel of mine, I am here. I know you are there. Put your wings around me and help me grow. Help me fly!" Practice dismissing bitterness, blame, fear, guilt, resentment, pain, and irritations from your daily life. These reactions in your thinking and emotions didn't build overnight. They took some repeating and reinforcing. Throwing them out will take some work, too. The junk in the basement isn't going to get up on its own. Go up the stairs and out the door to the dump! You are going to have to bend, lift, sort, climb, haul, and sweep up! But oh, the satisfaction of having it cleaned up. Now you have room for some new, fresh, exciting, colorful, creative, and positive stuff. All the while, the love and encouragement is hovering about you and cheering you on.

Honestly, this is the way it is! How could it be otherwise, when you are a part of the pure, bright, and endless energy of the God or All love? It is yours. And it is due you. So love, be about your days on your trip to Earth. Keep paying off those karmic debts. Do it as joyfully as possible. Imagine that you have won the lottery, and are now going from place to place to pay your debts in cash! You know you have more than enough money to do so. You may even add a trip here and there to add to your dharma bank at home, like one for good measure.

How great is it when another says to you, thank you, I'm sorry, I forgive you, I miss you, I need you, I want you, or I love you? You are comforted, right? You feel good, right? So does the other person. It's not hard to identify what you are fixing, working on, and correcting during this life, with another person, situation, or group. It is usually difficult or uncomfortable. The person who annoys you to no end is there for a reason. Think about it.

Walk Out, Walk In

Souls put themselves in lifetime situations and set up great tasks for themselves. It can happen that a soul takes on more than they can handle in one lifetime. No one stops you at Home, as you write your script. Fellow loving souls may advise you, but the end choice is yours. Those who choose to take on too much may become dear ones who can't seem to sort out what to do next. Can anyone help them to see that it doesn't all have to be accomplished in one lifetime? Can they be comforted? If not, to end a life before the time arranged creates more karmic debt. The ripples of pain project out into the Universe as an anguished scream.

There are some dear souls who do give up. They can't hang on and just want their pain to end. It may be a physical, mental, or emotional pain. Their despair is deep. They become blind and deaf to solutions and can't bear tomorrow. They use their freewill to end the life they chose to put in motion. Sometimes, no matter how much they are loved and cared for, they are in a mental and emotional pit. When these dear souls arrive home, they are welcomed lovingly, as is everyone. They rest a while until they can evaluate their choices. In their next life, almost always, they have very strong feelings against suicide.

There is another solution, or "soul-lution." There is another choice. Everyone has helpers everywhere, souls who love you and are at Home, at your service. It happens on occasion, that a soul close to ending their own energy on Earth, asks desperately for help from their higher, true self. They are connected to Home. It can happen that an agreement on a soul level is made, and the soul at Home slowly begins to send energy to the troubled soul in despair. It is more than a thought transfer. It is a blending of energies and shadowing from the soul at Home to the soul on Earth.

Over a period of years, they gradually balance their energies mentally, emotionally, and physically. It is not instantaneous or sudden, but they exchange places! It happens that some souls set up a life plan that is too much to handle and accomplish, or others damage them repeatedly. Their will to continue is depleted. There can be many different situations.

The soul at Home loves the Earth soul unconditionally, and accepts a tremendous task. It has the opportunity to skip the baby and childhood years. However, this soul studies the life plan of the Earth soul. Part of the bargain is to complete what the soul on Earth set up to do. They are like a stand-in. Another soul steps into your life, fuels your body, and finishes the script.

Over years, one walks out and one walks in or, more accurately, flows in. Once the "walk-in" has fulfilled the original script, they can then be about their own soul experiences and growth. This is not an easy transition. You may know people who have gone through a long period of difficulty, and very gradually end or change their way of living. Relationships are altered, even occupations. A huge transformation occurs in them. They go forward on an entirely different course.

This is not to be confused with men and women who put great energy, study, and struggle into turning their lives around and going forward on a different life path. How do you know?

You don't. Perhaps, in deep examination and meditation, an individual could identify that they chose this help, and made this deep contract with another soul. The walk-out does not "die," or pass over to Home. They are in a "waiting room," observing the walk-in and their life course. During the early years, there is constant communication on the soul level, while the walk-in gets used to the body, circumstances, and energies. The walk-out does not incur karma or dharma in this time, as each soul is individual and unique. The walk-in creates its own brownie points and demerits. When it is time for the walk-in to leave, and put the body down, they join again in agreement and gratitude. They go Home together! The walk-out did not incur karma for ending its life path through suicide and causing pain to others by this choice. The walk-out gave another soul an opportunity to grow through what he or she had already begun.

To another living a life around this person, the whole process can be invisible. There are usually adjustments in thinking and handling emotions. Sometimes, the physical body energy exchange is a hard balance to achieve. The walk-in may alter, in some ways, the walk-out's health or appearance. But this, too, can happen to all souls with constant change and having the use of all creativity. You don't know. The walk-in is a long studied and experienced soul to be able to accept this loving challenge. The walk-out is to be revered also, for accepting another source of love for themselves and others.

Have a Good Time

These examples and explanations seem so heavy! Don't lose sight of being on a vacation—a journey, an opportunity for advancement. You are not going to turn down the opportunity that a promotion at your job would give you. No, because you would gain from it. You are not going to reject an invitation to a party with interesting and fun people, and great eats. No, because it is an opportunity to meet new people, see and do something different.

Opportunities are openings to put your energy elsewhere and multiply it. Remember early on in this book, you got all your gear together—a map, money (energy), and friends—to travel to Earth to experience and explore? It is very important to keep uppermost in your mind that life on your gorgeous planet should not be all work and no play. In fact, the more fun you have, the better. It keeps your body healthy, your mind alert, and your soul bright. It is also an energy that draws fun people to you. People like to be with people who are easy to be around.

Very often, the debt and work of a life plan becomes such a burden, that all sights and ideas of fun are lost. Then there is an imbalance. After all, you and all souls like you have been working to make life easier through the centuries. Everything is easier than it was one or two hundred years ago, at least, for those of you in modern countries. Your every moment of every day is not concerned with keeping a fire lit and finding something to eat.

For many of you, the challenging tasks of the material things on Earth have been to make them serve your comforts, and save you time—to do what? More work? No, to play or to be still. Also, if you have more time, you can share it with others by serving them. Who doesn't live for a day off? The weekend? The holiday? Being with your loved ones and playing sends out positive energy vibrations that help balance many negative ones of hardship, harm, and misuse across the planet.

Your vacation on Earth is supposed to be fun. Moses, Mohammed, Jesus, Mother Theresa . . . all had fun here. They enjoyed laughing and talking. They were real flesh and blood and had emotions, like you. They were like all men and women. No one was going to listen to a cold robot. Think a minute.

When you have a problem, the last person you would go find to discuss it with, is the person who wouldn't understand you. You know they haven't any experience with what you are going through. Or you don't respect how they have conducted their life and they can't help you. Of course, you call, e-mail, or visit one that you know will embrace you, not judge you, and will help you look at and solve your problem.

Well, all the teachers we know in written history had to live a lot to understand what people were thinking, feeling, and struggling with in their day. They walked among others. A smile, a laugh, nice words, trust, and love drew people to them to hear their words. They taught through entertaining stories, as is still done. Earth souls are often enlightened through entertainment. Movies, TV, books, PCs, and CDs are all teaching tools. Laughter, joy, and fun are also the energies of Home. Positive energy flows. Negative energy pushes and pulls and forces. Your joy, peace, and contentment can come from the simplest acts, words, and deeds. Seek out others who lift your life. Then share with them. Laugh and play with them. Then, when the karma needs to be worked on, you have a store-house of positive energy to draw upon to do your chores. In sharing fun with others, you give them strength to meet their opportunities to pay their debts.

Friends at Home

Not every energy spark chooses to explore other places from Home. Some decide to observe all the creating going on and to be there to help out when needed. These souls have not placed their energy in a physical Earth body. They are Angels. Home is a busy dimension. A lot is happening. Energy is flowing constantly. Picture the travel agency where souls are deciding on their next adventure. Should I go to Earth, other planets, or other galaxies? What will I wear? Who will go with me? What location is best? I'll plan an itinerary and return time.

Picture the "Homecoming" committee. When souls from earthquakes and disasters come Home in big groups, or as individuals from their deathbeds, the word is sent out of their return Home so loved ones can meet them, like at the airport. Picture a special resting place for every single, special soul at Home, like a permanent embrace and gentle sleep. Much like the baby on Earth in loving arms who just has to be who they are, and are loved for who they are. Nothing is required of them but to sleep, eat, and grow. The baby is watched over. It is in a little limbo, while it adjusts to Earth life. All of its needs are met. And it is so with the soul that has come Home. It rests and is allowed to be who it is. It is watched over and loved until it is ready to reawaken.

Picture many circles of lights, souls on all different levels, like a high-rise building. Some are in "welcome home" classes, being reminded of their true identities. Some are studying colors, numbers, harmony, and energy. Some are in group-thought to send love to troubled groups and difficult situations on Earth and other planets. Some work with babies and children, who chose to live short lives on Earth and need reminders of their script's mission. Some use their energy to monitor the air, waters, gases, and planets. There are teachers, students, and all degrees of accomplishment. Everyone is about becoming. No one is wrong or bad or evil. There is no end to the possibilities.

Picture the "computer room" with the Akashic records, the original videotapes of you and yours. There are souls who are the record keepers without judgment, just the facts—with love. When you are rested and ready, you can check out your own autobiography of how you used your energy. Did you follow your script? How did you do if you had to detour? Did you pile up some dharma? Did you make up to others what you owed them? Did you have fun? How did you do? Then you can think about it, as long as you want, and enjoy Home. If you need to learn and experience more and have another Earth life, you think about it and plan for the right time for you and others involved.

Picture the best theme park ever. Imagine vast beauty. Gorgeous music. Anything you can think of is yours, and your thoughts bring it to you. Knowledge and all teachers are at your service. You share your experiences. Everyone is a teacher. Language cannot describe the utter limitless, endless, vastness of Home. What one can think, it can be. Many souls have done a lot of thinking in all of creation. Some of what you have seen in many movies about Home is true. It has been remembered and the ideas have been re-created in books so that you, too, may remember.

Picture the information booth with soul guides that have direct phone lines to Earth souls in service. The Earth soul suspends their personality, like stepping in another room, while the guide at Home borrows their body to teach through. This is called channeling or shadowing. It is for a brief time. Everyone has his or her own guide and soul energy at Home. You can "call them up" on your own phone in prayer or meditation. Be still. Let them flow to you. Have you ever had a new idea just pop into your head? Often, it is your guide, Angel, or higher-self sending you what you need. "Ask and you shall receive. Be still and know that you are God." This is a tiny dent of a description of your true Home. To some, when they get Home, they remember right away. Others need a little time, then go, "Oh yeah, now I remember."

New, Old, and Wonderful Souls

There are new souls, young souls, and old souls. All are equal; they are simply in different stages of experience. A new soul is one that has just begun experiencing the Earth-school. "New soul" does not mean newly formed, but new experiences. New souls are often those in tribal situations, just getting started. Young souls refer to those who have experienced much, but do not yet have the big picture and the conscious idea that we are all one. Old souls have been around the planet and often other planets a few times. They have the big picture and know that we are all a part of one another. They have lots of experience, knowledge, and wisdom. They can be teachers or just a simple, sweet, good example.

New, young, and old souls have equal choices in their freewill. That is, there is always room for right use and misuse of energy no matter who you are. All energies in all galaxies and planets are responsible for the right use of energy. Some misuses have been, for example, travelers from other galaxies interfering with Earth bodies, or soul energies giving information that would influence choices. There is good use and misuse of all tools. A palm reader, for instance, could "read" and say aloud that you could die young. This is a huge interference with the person's freewill and future choices. Occasionally, doctors tell people they are terminally ill but the tests turn out to be wrong. Mentally, this person lives differently under this cloud. This is an interference with a person's flow of energy.

You also hear of "saints." These are wonderful souls in history, who were good examples to all they lived among. Their examples of faith and sacrifice would be remembered; they were given, so to speak, the "academy award." They were ordinary folk, flesh and blood, who had a mission to show others how to love and live. Religious groups designated them "saints." There are criteria these souls had to meet in order to be considered a saint. Mother Theresa of Calcutta, India, was a shining example of unconditional love. She walked the path daily of selflessness and gave of herself with joy. She was accepting and loving of all—from the most desperate and deprived souls, to the most privileged and advantaged souls. She truly saw all men and women as one energy. This is "saintly."

But all saints are not world figures or well known. There is one at the checkout at the grocery, or living down the street, or in your family, or club. They ooze tolerance, acceptance, and are quiet reminders to everyone through their good example. Look for them. Maybe you are one. Everyone's soul light shines brightly. Sometimes, it is just hidden by layers of negative energy. It is each person's challenge to look past those layers to recognize and appreciate the good in every soul you meet. Often, they themselves don't know it's there. Maybe it is in your script to remind them.

Men and women are with one another in situations for a reason. It may be for a moment, a day, a year, nine years, or a lifetime. Just as no one else knows your plans, you don't know those of others. What you observe in relationships is the cream on top. You don't know what is holding it up. Be, speak, and think kindly—the same kindness that you would appreciate.

Keep in mind that some very evolved, knowledgeable, and experienced souls may be "under cover" as a very average person of education, who makes seemingly endless mistakes and unwise choices. But, yet, they shine. Through all their errors, they demonstrate a genuine recognition of their oneness with everyone. This is the "role" they are to project to get attention and be noticed. In this day and age, one's quiet life in a village can, in moments, be projected to the whole planet and beyond. How painful would this be? To be watched, judged, talked about, and scrutinized. But, since some popular people are projected into everyone's lives, this may be their soul's intention. In some cases, it is a sacrifice to allow everyone to observe them and how they live. Through modern technology, you hear the most about political figures and entertainment people. Everyone is drawn to them and their lives. It is human nature to be nosey; it is "saintly" to not judge.

When people seem too perfect, other personalities label them and can't relate to them. They may be called a "do-gooder," "Pollyanna," or "goody-two-shoes." Instead of being seen as a positive, they are deemed negative and made fun of. This is because the struggling souls of men and women are challenged by them to do better, and most often, we don't want another "in our face" about what we should do, think, and be.

So, the stinker, the underdog, the bully with the good heart, appeals to more of us, because they seem more like us in their everyday lives. Well, guess what? In his day, Jesus was the odd guy, the "hippie." Contrary to most stories about him for two thousand years, he was not perfect. This thought may hurt your brain a little. How do you think he got noticed? By being different and by being very human. He had a personality that had to learn new ways, just as you. Envy, anger, selflessness, a work focus, discipline, temptation, pain, disappointment, betrayal, and fears all had to be worked through in this lifetime he chose, even though he was an evolved soul with a great mission.

The universal All, all of us, knew it was time to shake things up, to get people thinking in another way. The Jews were on the right track, but were getting bogged down in rituals and laws. The Romans were the wild guys, roaming all over the Earth and claiming places and peoples under their rule. These were two extremes in Jesus' time where he lived. All those years in his teens and twenties, he was out walking and talking. He was getting blisters on his feet, working for food in fields on his journey, asking questions, and seeking answers, just as you are. He put up with the heat, rain, bug bites, and souls in all places in their growth. He was ignored and rebuffed. He got tired, angry, disappointed, and nasty, at times, just as you do. He had to experience as much as he could in his short life. He became aware of his mission the older he got. His family, friends, and apostles set up their life plans to be a part of the universal agreement to jolt the thinking of men and women in this time period. They had shared previous lives together. They were soul mates together to support each other in fulfilling a shake-up in group consciousness.

Jesus chose not to have a personal, intimate love—no girl-friend, wife, or children. His energy was not split to have a help-soul in a twin flame. He needed his energy, full force, to concentrate on what he'd come to express and complete. Buddha left his wife. When one has a mate, it takes constant attention and a sharing of your energy. Mates can accomplish great things in their learning together, but some souls dedicate their energy to many others and can focus better by not being coupled. This is a choice that nuns, priests, monks, and others make to learn and serve.

What Did Jesus Do?

He met danger from the elements, animals, and men on his walk. It was a long walk. He had time to think, time to connect to his higher self and remember who he was and why he chose this lifetime. He questioned his life and mission. He learned, day by day, to get to his last day. He had to walk the imperfect steps of man, since he was a man. He didn't really want to be beaten, spit at, and crowned with thorns and nailed to a cross, which was the punishment of the day. I am sure he would have preferred lethal injection. But then, who would have paid attention if he'd died in his sleep or of the flu? He had to make an impact, so everyone would keep talking about him. Men and women sure have, for over two thousand years now.

His mission was to give you an example. For you to think, "Gee, he was betrayed by his best friends and he forgave them. I can try to forgive as well." Jesus said, "If I don't have to be crucified, I'd rather not." Everyone thinks this way when confronted with something difficult that they must do.

Follow your path, not that of others. Temptations are all around you—it is life in all its variety. We can physically die and leave the body, but we live again and are resurrected at Home. Over and over, one has a chance and choice to do better, to be better to one's self and to others. Jesus did his best. You do your best. Do not compare yourself to him or any other. Be and become. You have what it takes and all the help you want. "Ask and receive." The Universe never says no.

There is a movement in the year two thousand plus, which is a fine reminder to think before you speak or act. It is a mental training to think, "What would Jesus do?" or you can replace Jesus with the Dalai Lama, Buddha, Gandhi, Moses, or Mother Theresa. This is a good idea, because one is reminded when thinking, "I am not perfect. I am becoming and learning, just as Jesus and the teachers did. I learn from my choices and share my lessons. I call on my higher self and all the energies there to help me to do the right thing. To use my energy positively."

No one on the Earth-school is ever perfect. Even all the above-mentioned, great, giving souls were not perfect. If they were, there would have been no need for them to put their energy into an Earth body form and attend the Earth-school. Sometimes, the models to follow are too extreme for us to be like. Instead of trying, mankind ignores them and gives up. Everyone must realize that perfection is not attainable on Earth. It can't be. There are too many wild and different energies zapping about to dodge and deal with.

Try and take the best of the people and examples you admire. It is easier to realize that they are like you or have been like you. What you see in them, you want to be. They, too, struggled to attain their qualities. This idea sure eliminates jealousy, greed, and criticism. You will be who you want to be. Your soul does grow in time. Trust this. It is faith in your use of energy.

Remember, Jesus was one of many teachers from the All. He was no more or less than Mohammed, Buddha, and the other teachers. Since this book that you are reading is available in the North American continent first, more references, descriptions, and examples of Jesus' life are presented. He is the teacher that most people in this region know, recognize, and follow. Try to think of Jesus as universal, a teacher for all men and women. We are all the same energy. Each teacher spoke to different groups at different times in history. They all established the same guidelines, just in different languages in different parts of the world.

After Jesus' travels, he went back Home, full of new ideas to use and test along the way. He needed people to listen. For many, their soul timing was right to be open-minded and to accept his teachings of: Love One Another, One Energy, A Father Image, Everyone is the Same, Healing, and Forgiveness. Just as now, your timing is right to have picked up this book to gain a new idea of who you are and what you and your fellow men and women are doing here. One does better if one understands the world and energies around them. You have opened a door to let some new ideas in. Leave it open now and know that there is nothing to fear.

"Cult," from "Culture," has become a dirty word, a negative thought usually about a group we don't understand and, therefore, are sometimes afraid of. Know that Jesus and his buddies were considered a "cult" in their day. Just because some people think, speak, and believe differently, does not mean they are evil or bad. To judge such people makes you no different from those in Jesus' day who said, "Well, we don't understand this guy, so let's kill him."

Be still, and when confronted with what you don't like or understand, know that there is room, need, and reason for all thought. One soul energy cannot know the plans, paths, and complexities of all men. Just know that you are a part of all men and women, and allow them their expression. To be tolerant of their choices is to be your very best, your true self. It is not easy to cement this idea in your heart, mind, and soul. As every day, everyone struggles with deception, hurt, injustice, fear, evil, meanness, and all aspects of negative choice in use of energy.

It is up to you to confront this misuse of energy, influence it, and change it to positive use. You can do it, fix it, and change it. Remember, all power and help is available to you. Seek it, find it, and use it! Your guardian Angel is counting on you. This is why they asked me to write you, to remind you of your mission.

There is a little thing you also need to know. Negative energy, the devil, or evil energy does exist. Picture Angels of light and Angels of darkness. Your guardian Angel is an Angel of light and your switchboard operator to your higher self and best energy. Your Angel reads the map for you when you are lost. He or she interprets confusing information and makes it clear for you. Your Angel serves your needs but cannot make your choices. This Angel also cannot stop the choice of an Angel of darkness from trying to influence your choices, because these Angels also have freewill. They, too, are a part of the All, so when temptations and influences come to you, and you feel weak and misuse your energy, your Angel of light can only watch, wait, and see what you decide. He or she hopes you have love of yourself and others to make right choices in your benefit. Your guardian Angel can't throw himself between you and an Angel of darkness and say, "Oh no you don't! Leave my Bob alone!" He has to buck up and say, "Okay, go ahead. Together, we'll see how Bob handles this." Then, no matter what Bob decides to do, his guardian Angel is there, forever waiting, ready to serve. The Angel of darkness won't be there. He or she doesn't have time or energy to waste. The Angel of darkness moves on to the next soul to try and *sap* their energy.

My Dear Ones: are you remembering more and more, who you are? I hope so. This is the purpose of this book. Everyone does better when they know what their plan is. Won't it be wonderful, one day, when the group, mass consciousness has evolved? When we all approach one another and treat one another like precious, valuable, gorgeous beings? Instead of saying, "Hi, how are you?" you may say, "How are you doing on your karma?" Or "Have you piled up lots of dharma?" Or, "What are you working on in this life mission? Can I help you?" Wow. Everyone would be more understanding of their family, friends, and life plans. The language is changing very slowly. The right ideas are out and about.

REMEMBER . . .

- Try to understand all people.
- Tolerance keeps an open mind.
- The Second Coming is YOUR awakening.
- Walk-ins trade places.
- Have lots of fun. Love more.
- There are many souls at Home that can help.

- New, young, and old souls all grow at their own pace.
- Wonderful souls have experiences to teach.
- Cult is not a dirty word.
- Angels of light and darkness are at your service or disservice.

Chapter 20

Answering Your Questions!

What Is My Purpose Here?

Your purpose here is to follow the script of your life, which you wrote, to the best of your ability. Experience Earth life, have fun, and strive to perfect your soul in all areas. Correct and repay debts to those you have harmed or been unjust to, or those you did not treat as you would yourself. Express love and reach the peak of knowledge that you are truly, divinely, one of and a part of, all beings and all things, as they are a part of you. To right a wrong to another is to right a wrong to yourself. You are one.

Is There Life after Death?

Of course. Life never ends. It just changes form. Life after an Earthly body death is lighter, totally free, and just heavenly. You go Home, after your Earth life, to where you are pure, a free spirit, and completely loved and comfortable. An example: When you go on a trip on Earth, you like to go home once it is over. Home is where your "stuff" is, your energy source. You are safe, comfortable, and familiar at home, with your routine, in your own bed. You are with people you love most and who love you. It is the same when you put the Earth body down. After all, you have "died" many times before and here you are again! Hooray for you. You are an explorer, a creator, and have lots you want to do. Life energy is forever and ever, beyond and then some. There is no end. Sometimes, you are a bright light. Sometimes, you are a dim light. Sometimes, you sparkle or flash. You choose. You are, as always, becoming!

There is also sex after death. However, without bodies, it is not like sex on Earth. There is a movie called "Cocoon" that shows beautifully the blending of energies. Only at Home, it is better yet! That's because there's no time, no space restrictions, no weight, or question of love. The people who wrote and made this movie remembered this to depict it so beautifully.

Why Do Bad Things Happen?

Not just bad things, but sometimes horrible, deplorable things happen—sad and tragic, frightening and fierce. These "things" often happen because you chose them to occur in your life plan, in order to challenge yourself and the past lessons you've learned, and to provide what your soul energy needs to work on and perfect. An example: You learn to play a card game. You play and play, yet never win. Finally, you do win. You love the feeling. Well, then you don't want to stop. You want to play again, to see if you really can win—really have learned the strategy and know it so well that you can teach it to another. (And to repeat the euphoria, and the thrill of winning.)

There may be awful things that occur in your life to you or to those around you. You may even have chosen to "sacrifice" a lifetime in order for others to learn. The brain-damaged child, the paralyzed adult, the homeless, and the dangerous may all be souls here just for you to learn from. They agreed to be in your life, to help you learn an important lesson. It could be for a short while, or long lifetime. It depends on how you set it up. Financial burdens, health issues, job problems, love not returned, misuse of alcohol, drugs, and one not understanding their role in their own script, are and can be "bad" things. These are also challenges, lessons, and experiences you chose to live and work through in order to perfect your ability to love and understand yourself and those around you.

Sometimes, people can get in the way of another's negative choice, which is not their creation or in their plan. There is a "being in the wrong place at the wrong time." If one is attuned to their intuition, some of these life plan-altering circumstances could be averted. Your script can be altered or erased by another misusing their energy. They are then responsible and must make it up to you in this life or another. The soul who did not take responsibility for a misuse of energy is one who yet does not realize and remember that he or she is first, last, and always a part of everyone else. If they did, they would not have harmed you in the first place.

Is There Intelligent Life Elsewhere?

Yes, indeed. In fact, everywhere! All creative life ideas expand, change, and evolve. At one time, you weren't so bright! There are yet Earth-plane persons who are just beginning, and have a long way to go. Where are you in your soul evolvement?

Intelligence is one thing. Men and women can get full of themselves, thinking they are so smart. Too much focus is placed on one's thinking advancement. They forget the everlasting spiritual, soul energy, advancement. Some are caught up in their bodies and place great emphasis here. This may be a need one may express, through extreme emotions and exercises, to entertain or instruct. Education and knowledge is vital, yet balance in all of these areas is the key to growth.

You will put down the body, the emotions, the personality, and your education. What keeps on going is your spiritual-soul energy. All of the above work together in a beautifully woven picture of creative experience. You have a right to "play" with the body and mind and emotions. After all, you created it as your own special vehicle through which to express.

Men and women on Earth are intelligent and advancing.

Your humanness wants to be better, superior. This keeps you hopping to learn and strive for more. No matter how "brilliant" you may be in this life, remember that in many previous lives, you were just plain dumb or perhaps more brilliant. Since other energies from other galaxies can whisk in and out of yours, you think this makes them intelligent. They are different. Where they live, they have their own stages of evolvement. Their space vehicles may be as ordinary to them as riding in a car is to you. No big deal. Their true intelligence may be spiritual. They may know that you on Earth are a part of them, and are about your own creative adventure, as is your right.

Since "they" are also becoming, some of "them" have misused their know-how to interfere with some of you on Earth. This was wrong use and has been corrected. When Earth souls return Home, they will understand this. These people must ask themselves, "Have I not been curious about others and interfered with their lives?" As I have said before, Earth is neither the kindergarten of the galaxy, nor is it the doctorate program. But it does not matter, as you chose the best spot for you to be and learn. All energies are a part of the All, just in different stages of becoming.

How Long Will I Live?

You will live on the Earth plane as long as you need to, in order to complete your lessons in your own soul growth. You could be an infant for only a few days, then leave your little body here and go back Home. On a consciousness level, in this brief time, you could have been of great service. You may have needed to experience some infancy problems to wrap up some aspect of learning. Remember, my Beloved, you write the story of you. You can choose the ending. Each is unique and has its own purpose.

Some souls seem very close to leaving, and stay longer.

Others are fine one moment, and headed Home the next. Many choose illnesses to experience for themselves and as lessons for others. You are in command. If you want to "die" in your bed, keep thinking that this is your plan and desire. Do not draw danger, fear, or tragedy to yourself. When your loved ones leave in floods, plane crashes, volcanoes, explosions, earthquakes, freak accidents, and at the choice of others, try and understand that they may very well have planned it. You all have to get out of your bodies in someway. So far, we have not designed the body to last a long time on Earth. Of course, we could.

Your seventy, eighty, or ninety-year life span is like your being away for a weekend to those at Home. It is as if you say, "Save my seat, I'll be back." And then, you are. It is very hard for you to imagine, since there is no time at Home. Think a moment, in the All of perpetual eternity, eighty years is a blink. You will see and remember when you are Home again. There is nothing to fear. You are so loved! Know without a doubt, that you are a part of the souls that stay at Home here. When you take your last breath, get ready for another great adventure.

Once you have experienced all you wish, and recognize yourself in your fellow men and women, you can stay Home. No need to put yourself in an Earthly body again, unless you want to. You may think, "Gee, I could have been tall, dark, handsome, rich, and had a V-8!" Of course, you could have. After all, each time, you risk weak moments, and misuse possibilities, and create karma. Or you could return to just walk the Earth and be a good example. This has been done, too. A time comes in soul evolvement when you feel you've "been there, done that." The soul then wants to serve or create anew. Your experience is whatever you want and desire. Thoughts are real things, remember?

There are many worlds to explore, many different life

forces to experience. Home loves all its guides and helpers who assist and promote their fellow souls coming, going, and staying. It is a career choice at home. When you are ready to move on at Home, you could do this, too.

There are many awful ways to leave the body, but the split second the soul energy plug is snapped, it is done and you're on your way. No more pain or fear. It is finished and released. The trip is over. Time then to unpack, rest up, get the photos developed, and tell everyone about your trip. They, too, learn from your trip experiences. Always, you are sharing, influencing, and giving, and the same comes to you.

Think about the following. If you were sitting or standing, stark naked, on the planet, alone, you would start creating. You would think of something to do or something to make. One thing would lead to another. You can't help but create. It is what you are—a creative energy with any and every idea at your disposal. Well, of course, this is where it all began in the first place, with one creative idea. All ideas are not good ideas, like the dinosaurs, but they have their testing time. Since the beginning flash of time, ten billion years ago—for reference sake, because there was no beginning—it is yet possible to have a new idea. So, think people, think. It's never over, so enjoy the flow.

Live and Learn, Live and Learn, Live and Learn

By now, you know deep down and deep within, that you are eternal and in control of all your days and all your choices. It is too limiting to think of one lifetime. How scary, to have one shot at an experience. When men and women like and enjoy something, they want to do it over and over again. The freedom of your choice is pretty darn powerful. You are only limited by the censors and stops that you put on your own imagination.

Pretend you are a feather pillow that can walk. Your ideas

and thoughts, love and essence, is all in the feathers in your pillowcase. Imagine you, the pillow, walking up a steep hill. At the top, it is windy. You feel the wind blowing and pushing at your pillowcase. All that you are is contained. Now, imagine opening the pillowcase and allowing all the feathers, your ideas, love, desires, dreams, and plans—the essence of you—out to blow in the wind. They blow where each aspect of you may explore the Universe. How refreshing the flow is. How open and free. What fun to release all the potential of you. And, just as you could never gather and contain all those feathers again, so you cannot end. You are eternal, ongoing, energy and love. Feel it, believe it, know it. You are your creator and un-creator. What you can make, you can remake. What you have misused, you can fix. You are always learning and exploring every moment of every single day. You are very wonderful. Allow others to see this beauty in you. Make an effort to always see it in others.

Why Do People Act That Way?
Every single soul has a story. A his-story and her-story. Mankind constantly finds one another interesting. The core of everyday life is to hear about one's day and one's experience. Some are magnified in books, movies, newspapers, and magazines. What did "so and so" do next? What was she thinking? Why did he do this or that? And now that you have explored beyond the physical and the personality of your fellow men and women, you can see lifetimes from a whole new and true perspective. You might now think about people you meet . . .

- "Oh, what are they wanting to accomplish this life?"
- "My, such a good person adding dharma to their soul account."
- "That dear soul is suffering. What is going on in their life plan?"

- "I am so glad that I am not her, and don't have to experience those circumstances."
- "Well, so much abundance must be due them. They earned this lifestyle."
- "Look at this fellow soul in service through their example. How difficult. How good he is to serve in this way."
- "I don't like their life." (Maybe this is because I struggled so to change this very thing in my life at some time.)
- "How can they have eight children?" (They must have relationships to round out with all these souls.)
- "He is so mean and abusive!" (Where does this pain and anger come from to be expressed so negatively?)
- "They are poor, beautiful, smart, simple, odd." (And all are a part of me, living a life they need to experience and learn through.)
- "Why is there violence and loss in their life?" (You don't know what energies proceeded this lifetime to create this story.)

To look beyond the physical person and bypass the playful personality, is to rise above and look into the soul energy that generates the choices and lifestyle. It is good to get in the habit of doing this. Think how often you sure would have liked someone to see the best in you, despite your actions, words, and personality games. Practice this. It will open a whole new flow of understanding to you. Maybe we'll even hear these future pickup lines . . .

- "You look like you're working on beauty this life."
- "That's a great body you created."
- "Have we met before, in a past life?"
- "What's your karma? Can I help?"

REMEMBER . . .

- Perfect your loving and your life on Earth.
- Death is temporary. Life never ends.
- Sex after death is good.
- Bad things may come from hard lessons that need to be learned.
- Intelligent life is everywhere.
- Not alien—Different!
- Live on Earth as briefly or as long as you want. You write your own Earth ending.
- Naked people can have new ideas!
- When your soul is awake, it sees others in different ways.

Chapter 21

Mysteries and Sharing Souls

Mysteries Solved

Since I am your Angel, I can see the "big picture" of life clearly. I am also a teacher Angel, so I have access to information that I have permission to share with you as learning examples. With this in mind, I will share some answers to "mysteries," for fun, with you. We all learn from each life experience. For the scientific and analytical mind, yes or no answers will leave you wanting for proof and details. Perhaps once you have the answer you can backtrack and fill in the blanks in your questions. You chose your exploring personality and questioning mind for this reason. Be aware that, from universal questions to answers to mysteries, man in body form cannot know and comprehend everything. Nor was he meant to. And, you do not need to know everything! Since creation is ongoing by all of us, there is no "catching up" with every detail of ideas.

In truth, the following are the outcomes of lives and situations mostly known in your area of the Earth. What really happened to . . . and what about . . . ?

- Jimmy Hoffa—He didn't expect this to happen to him, but was murdered.
- Amelia Earhart—The crash made her more famous than she ever would have been in life. There were mechanical problems and soon, evidence of this will be found.
- President John F. Kennedy—He was killed through a conspiracy. He has gone on in soul growth at Home.

- The Shroud of Turin—This cloth has on it the imprint of Jesus the Christ. He was physically changed as he went through a purification process before he died and was very thin.
- Noah's Arc—The Arc did exist and was not just a Bible story.
- Crop Circles—Some were made by extraterrestrials.
- The Loch Ness Monster—Sorry, a fun idea, but it is not there.
- Marilyn Monroe—This sweet soul died accidentally. She was in despair and made a mistake. She will return to the Earth soon.
- The Space Challenger—These lives were cut short due to a mechanical accident.
- Stonehenge—A community effort of men built this for a weather alignment, for their survival.
- The Unicorn—This horse-like animal did exist and became extinct. Once the blueprint for any animal creation is destroyed, man loses the right to have it again and karma is created.
- The Anti-Christ—He or she is not on the Earth now—a negative energy guide to those who accept the energy. It is an energy that focuses on itself.
- Satan—The original bad guy has been transformed and has attained leaps in soul growth.
- John F. Kennedy, Jr., Carolyn Bessette Kennedy, and Lauren Bessette—The plane crash was in the life plan of all three to leave early. John was a very evolved soul and his life was to serve as a good example. He achieved a great deal in not using his looks, money, and charm selfishly.
- A Man on the Moon?—Some people are adamant about debunking the space mission to land a man on the

moon. This shows the power of perception. Often, no matter what the facts are, one denies the facts because they insist on their perception. We here at Home watched the men land and walk on the moon. It was very exciting. The footprints are there.

- The Lindbergh Baby—The real kidnapper of Charles Lindbergh's baby was not caught. He has made his transition Home. There was a terrible miscarriage of justice as Bruno Hauptmann was at the wrong place at the wrong time. Had he spoken English and been an American, he would not have been charged in the baby's kidnapping and death. At Home, he has overcome the trauma and mistaken judgment of him. At that time, there was a public outcry when Lindbergh's baby was taken. This was good and people should feel outraged and do what they can to help to be of service when anyone is being treated badly. People often pull back because it is painful and they don't want to watch. When you see harm being done, step forward and try to stop it.

- The Bermuda Triangle—There are many energy "hot spots" on the planet since it is made of energy. Some "spots" or areas on your body are "hotter" and more active than others. (Your heart pounds. Your toes just hang on.) In the Western United States there are some energy "hot spots" people know of that they go to and use for healing. The Bermuda Triangle was well documented by sailors long ago. Travelers into the area knew of the risks for obliteration because of the powerful energy. Some got too close and were caught and some said they were and weren't. This energy spot is dwindling now and will become a place of stories. Eventually, this energy will be gone.

- About Mysteries—Some unsolved mysteries involving people yet on Earth cannot be discussed. This would be interfering with the involved people's life lessons and privacy. Just as you may not want another to reveal what karma you are working through, we will respect our fellow men and women's right to experience, whether it is right use or misuse.

Sharing Souls

People learn from one another. This is a smart thing to do. Some dear souls, who were well known on the Earth-school, have volunteered to share with you their lifetime experiences. They, too, are a part of you and know that one soul's gain is a universal gain for our energy of one. Just as you may tell friends to do or not do something because of your good or bad experiences, your fellow souls are sharing their lifetime goals, plans, and purpose, and what happened to them. Remember that they are Home, so have had time to see the big picture of their soul experience, and their place on the planet stage.

Marie Curie—1867-1934

Marie Curie discovered radium, an important factor in modern medicine. Born Maria Sklodowska in Warsaw, Poland, she chose to be female and came to a father who taught science. Marie had "looked" Polish and this was an oppressed group at this time. The University of Krakow would not admit her to science studies, because she was a woman. She went to the Sorbonne University in Paris, because they encouraged women scientists. She spoke French, and France was sympathetic to the Polish people.

Marie met Pierre Curie in a science lab at the Sorbonne University. They married in 1895 and made scientific research their mutual life work. They also had two daughters. Credit goes to Marie for discovering radium, which kills bacteria such as typhus, cholera, and anthrax. Overwork with radium experiments caused Madame Curie's health to fail. The experiments were very dangerous. Enormous skill and judgment was necessary in order to extract the radium from pitchblende. One ton of pitchblende yielded, with luck, six grains of radium! In 1922, she won the Nobel Prize in Chemistry. Her daughter and son-in-law carried on her work.

To you, she says: "Before I came to the Earth, I had observed the energies and knew I wanted to study science and the energies of how things worked on Earth. I had chosen the male body many lifetimes before, because being male was easier, since men dominated the planet. I knew it would be more difficult as a woman. I loved France and still do. It was a home to me. They have a much more open attitude in many areas. For all the life difficulties I had, it was an extremely rewarding life, one of academic achievement, and soul achievement. This life was an absolute boost for my soul growth, as it was a life in service, even though I died as a result of my work.

"I needed to learn about being female. As most of the culture did at this time, women were not regarded as intellectually superior to men. Previously, as a man, I did not regard women as beings with intelligence. So, as a woman, and scientist, I was able to show the truth that women are equal and intelligent. It was a step forward for females and for science."

Ludwig Von Beethoven—1770-1827
Ludwig Von Beethoven's whole being breathed beauty in sound. At about thirty years of age, he became deaf and produced some of his greatest works in the years after, "hearing" them only in his brain. Ludwig was born in Bonn, Germany. He chose a tyrant of a father, who sang as a tenor. He

recognized his son's musical gifts and kept him constantly at his musical studies. His father knew that music was Ludwig's real work, and found teachers for him. At twelve, Ludwig was conducting an opera. He thought, felt, and dreamed in tones. He had exactitude in composing. His parents died, and he was invited to Vienna, Austria to study. He became eccentric and odd, slovenly and rude. His music was beautiful; his personality was a mess. After he became deaf, he went through a time of despair and depression. He finally became resigned to his deafness and went on with his work and life with his many friends.

To you, he says: "I'll bet you wouldn't guess it was karmic that I was deaf? I chose it to work through. Music is my passion and one of the aspects of soul growth that I have used, because it is so important. The vibrations of music tie to the vibrations of all the different energies of all the planets, Universes, and galaxies. Music is very important and I chose deafness to challenge myself, and to go on writing music in my head. It was a great achievement for me.

"I was so obsessed with the music that growth in my personality was ignored. I have had to work on other lifetimes since to be more receptive of people. This lifetime was a truly great experience. It was absolutely wonderful to work with music and to compose. The deafness was a small price to pay, to achieve the soul growth that I did.

"My next lifetime didn't have music in it. I chose India and a short life in a diseased area. I knew it would be brief, but I needed to learn aspects of being a child in this culture. Then another opportunity appeared that would give my soul more rounding out. It, too, was brief in a Northern and cold country. I had an opportunity as a walk-in, to help a young woman that was pregnant without marriage, and her soul was in anguish. She wanted to step away (die). It was important that this child be born, as he had much to contribute to his community. I got to step in to help her, and experience the birthing process. It was very interesting. The mother and I then went Home. Since then, I have been here, at Home, and listening to music and to different composers and it's all wonderful. Music is the language of the soul."

Judy Garland—1922-1969

On June 10,1922, Frances Ethel Gumm was born to theatre entertainers. Later known as Judy Garland, from age thirteen, she was a dancer, singer, and actress. She starred in the movies *Meet Me In St. Louis, The Hardy Boys Series, The Ziegfield Follies*, and *The Wizard Of Oz*, among others—thirty-five films in all. In spite of giving audiences much joy through her talents, she became dependent on drugs and alcohol and suffered from depression, emotional upsets, and self-doubt. Judy Garland had three children: Liza Minelli, and Lorna and Joe Luft.

She says to you: "When I got back Home, it took a while for me to be comfortable. My energy was very scattered, as my Earth lifetime had been very painful. Recently, new information has come out about me in the media. It is truth.

"I chose a very difficult lifetime, from my choice of parents and my childhood to many life choices. There was a lot of deception and misuse present in my life, and it was used against me by people I was supposed to be able to trust. Because of the drugs in my system, it took a while to acclimate myself at Home. Though my body was gone, the drugs affected me mentally, and the memory is still strong in my soul. I rested and dear souls would visit me to teach me where I was, and to help me remember that I was here before. I now feel contentment and have gone to many classes. I listen to spiritually-based music.

"My main regret is in leaving the lifetime as soon as I did.

It was not planned to return Home so soon. I had set up a few more years on the Earth, but was able to accomplish much of what I wanted. There was an accident that sent me Home too soon.

"I regret not having more time with my daughters and son. There was so much scattered energy in my life, that some goals were not accomplished. I'll be Home for a while, before I decide to return to the Earth. I want more time to study here. There is a whole area here that works with spiritually-based sound and harmony. I am very attracted to it, as I was a student here before I lived as Judy Garland.

"I chose a difficult and abusive childhood. I wanted to perform and be an entertainer, as I thought this would bring me much joy. It brought some, but it brought more to other people. (The energy of love continues on.) I want my children to know that I am with them, love them, and wish that we'd had more time together."

Marquis de La Fayette—1757-1834

The Marquis de La Fayette was a Frenchman who inherited a large fortune when orphaned at age thirteen. He chose the Army for his career. In 1777, he traveled to America to help the colonists against the British. He became one of George Washington's efficient soldiers. He was a brilliant strategist and was awarded in thanks by the U.S. Congress with $200,000 and 24,000 acres. In France, La Fayette was a commander of the National Guard and supported order and the Constitution. He opposed Napoleon and left public life until the monarchy was restored in 1815. He was a supporter of liberal ideas and until he died, worked to counteract the King's non-liberal ideas.

He says to you: "Some writings have said that I had an ulterior motive in helping the colonies become established. This is not true. I helped in the fight and was drawn to the idea of freedom on the Earth, as I know freedom from Home. This is why I took up the cause. It was not my heart's desire to have there be freedom for everyone. When in body form, I was raised to think that the aristocracy was higher than mankind. Then I died, and went Home, and remembered how off-the-wall this idea is.

"When I returned to the Earth, I had the opportunity to help establish the United States. I did so, not to be important in my own country, or for the history books, or to be well received at court. I did it because I loved the idea of freedom and liked Ben Franklin and Daniel Webster. They were good friends, and this is where my heart was."

Anne Frank—1929-1945

Anne Frank was born June 12, 1929, in Frankfurt, Germany. In January 1933, after the Nazi takeover of Germany, Anne's father, Otto, moved his family to Amsterdam, Holland. He was director of a food company. In 1940, the Nazis occupied Holland and the Jewish children were separated to Jewish schools and forced to wear a yellow Jewish Star of David to identify them. Jews were being deported to the concentration camp, Auschwitz. Anne's father made a hiding place in the warehouse where he worked. They were supplied with food and necessities by her father's co-workers.

While in hiding for two years and four months with her parents, sister, a dentist friend, and a couple with their son, Anne kept a diary of her thoughts and everyday existence. When the Germans found their hiding place, her diary pages were thrown about. The co-workers found them and returned them to her father, Otto, when he returned to Amsterdam after the war, the only survivor of the group.

Anne Frank: The Diary of a Young Girl was published.

Anne's writing showed great talent of observation, originality, and description. She displayed the humor, hopes, and relationships of the eight in hiding and their fears of discovery. It was a record of their daily concerns with food, hygiene, and life under adverse conditions and dangerous circumstances. Anne's short life and diary insights have been an inspiration for many. Anne died of disease, starvation, and exhaustion at camp Bergen-Belsen a few weeks before the liberation.

All standards of sensibilities were voided as the prisoners were degraded to animal level in camps not designed for survival. She says to you: "I was not well known in my lifetime, but am now. I don't have anything to correct. I was very surprised to find out (here at Home), that I was famous because of my writing. I have heard much said that a possible famous writer was lost, because I died young. I want to tell you that it doesn't matter, as my death was no more important than anyone's. Man is diminished by the death of each one. The housewife's life down the street was just as important as mine and everyone else's. Many lives were cut short and no one's life was more valuable than another.

"Some have said a great author was lost, because what I wrote was so moving. I wrote what I saw, and what was in my heart, and how we were living. I am very grateful my story was published, so the world had a peek at what it was like, because it was very frightening, a very difficult situation to be in and live through. I am extremely grateful that I was able to do it, as I knew it would happen. It was part of my plan. But living through it was difficult.

"There is much love in my heart for all mankind. Much love. There were kindnesses in the concentration camp. Some of the German guards tried to be kind. They were not all monsters. It was not that way. This needs to be said. Even though what happened was wrong, they were not all mean and monsters. Some did small kindnesses secretly, or they would have been punished. This is something I want people to know."

Princess Diana Spencer—1961-1997

Diana was born into the inner circle of royalty in Great Britain. Despite this, she was ranked a commoner and became the first commoner to become a Princess since 1660. She married Charles, the Prince of Wales, the first son of the Queen of England, in 1981. With no higher education or career training, she became a one-woman public relations star for the royal family and Great Britain. A beautiful person, with a complex personality and flawed life made public at every turn, Diana rose above her personal betrayals, grief, and very human reactions. She walked in the steps of everyman with no privacy, and rose above it, giving herself to others and causes for mankind. Her life was like everyone else's despite her privilege. Diana showed everyone how to transform personal suffering by reaching out to others. Diana brought to the world two sons, William and Harry, and set them on their way. She died in August 31, 1997, in a car accident that shocked the entire planet. Her young death and mission were frozen in time. She was a modern teacher.

The royal family has a group karma. It will, in time, play itself out. Diana was a light, and was there to serve as an example to the world. Even though many negative words have been written about her personality, much of it is not true. She had an open, loving heart that she reached out with when she stepped onto the world stage. In her personal relationships, she was like an ordinary person. She had difficulties because of her childhood home situation. She wanted a stable and loving home and family. Her life plan was to be on the world stage, and to express through her physical beauty and loving heart. She chose to share a lifetime with Charles. They had been in lifetimes together before, and were working on life aspects together and they will probably be together again another time.

Diana was a shining example to the world of someone who was able to step forward in difficult times. There are many who miss her, love her, and wish she were still on Earth. Diana is Home and now conscious, after resting, and is missing her sons. This has been most difficult for her.

Three died that day, and made the transition Home. Much was said that she could have stayed. The decision to go Home had already been made. Dodi Fayed and Henri Paul died instantly, and Diana a short time later. She had a short life, but is a great old soul. She was an example of one stepping above the problems she had to deal with to be a source of love. In her heart, she was a mother first. She checks in on her sons and is happy to see them doing well. Had circumstances been different, she would have had more children. Diana will now be Home for quite a while. She works with young souls (infants) who come Home early. She remembers Home now and knows her way around.

Dodi Fayed and Henri Paul both agreed with her, before being born on Earth, to be participants in her (and their) passing. Trevor Rees Jones didn't have to be in the car, but he was very conscientious and wanted to make sure Diana was taken care of. He had great respect for her and really wanted to protect her. It has been devastating to him that Diana, Dodi, and Henri died, as his job was to serve and protect, and he wasn't able to do that. The circumstances were taken out of his control. It was not Trevor Rees Jones' time to go Home, nor part of his life plan.

Diana says to you: "I had to be an example. I was hopeful that being tormented by photographers would make it easier on other people. They seem to be better about my sons. I am hopeful for both of my boys, as much grief is still there. I have tried to put myself in dream passages to them, so they know that I am alive and joy-filled. I also don't have to die anymore, and this is good. I look and see here, how important it is that mankind is in service to mankind. I was to be an example of a real woman, with real problems. My goal was to express a loving heart. I was very concerned that William and Harry know how difficult life can be for people. I did not want their lives to be like Charles'. It was confusing for him that his parents were not attentive, yet gave him everything. I wanted my boys to be better grounded and balanced. I am watching them and I am joyful that this is happening.

"Even though I am Home, I will not sever my connection with William and Harry. I will always be a loving, healing source for them, until we are together again.

"Trevor Rees Jones was unfortunate enough to be in the car with us. His healing and concerns will take time, but he will release it. I know he thought I was with the wrong person. It was just our time to move on (and not his).

"The karma I was involved in working on was with Charles and the royal family. My connection with them goes back a couple hundred years. Camilla was not part of this karma. Her situation with Charles is something from a more recent time period."

Napoleon Bonaparte—1769-1821

Napoleon Bonaparte was the son of a Corsican lawyer. When he defied the united forces of Europe and became the emperor of France in 1804, he was called the "Little Corporal." The force of his domineering personality and military genius won him brilliant victories. He was also a statesman, an educator, and an administrator. He established, in France, the Napoleon codes of civil and criminal procedure, penal law, and commerce. These aspects of his life were his true glory and not that of later being called "the scourge of Europe" and winning forty battles. His soldiers' welfare was always his first concern. He respected and cared for them. His admirers and detractors regarded him as a great soldier though a dark Angel of destruction. He died on the island of Helena at age fifty-two of cancer.

Note: The request was put out on the ethers for any well-known souls who wished to share what they had learned in their lifetime. Dear Napoleon was insistent to speak though in his many years at Home, the opinion of many loving energies is that he has not made a lot of progress in his thinking. Note also that this is an example of the power of the personality overriding one's higher self in opening up to flexibility in regarding new ways and ideas. Even though the everlasting spirit has no physical body to have a "personality," the soul energy retains memory of the personality.

He says to you: "I was recently in the 1980s in the French Foreign Legion in Africa. I was autocratic in my personality and an excellent soldier and was well liked, but was disappointed when I did not move up in rank. In the lifetime as Napoleon, people adored or hated me. My country and soldiers were of utmost importance to me. My true love was France and my men. I did all I could to make it easier for them. That is why they loved me. This was a very physical life. Russia was a big mistake, as was Waterloo.

"It truly was not love on my part with Josephine. I was totally infatuated with her. She was no fool and decided when I was so persistent to marry me as it was a good match. She was a very intelligent woman. I was obsessed with her because she said 'no' all the time and I was not used to this."

Post Script from Home Angels . . . "Napoleon loves war and strategy. He yet has the idea that it is noble to bring all under the rule of France. He loves France. He has not moved on as he could have. In his most recent lifetime, however, he was more aware of his spirituality. He is taking classes here to move beyond warring. He needs to learn and grow as we all do."

Plato—429(?)-347(?) BC

Plato was a Greek philosopher, born in Athens, Greece. He was well educated and became associated with Socrates when he was twenty until Socrates' death. He was one of the great teachers of all time and devoted forty years to an academy he founded in Athens. Plato taught Aristotle and wrote the book *The Republic* and other teaching documents regarding politics, ethics, and education. He wrote against the decadence and corruption of Greece at the time. Plato observed and believed that the lowest education involved the visible world of art, literature, and natural things. Above this, comes the intellectual world of math, the abstract, and hypothesizing. Then, the highest form is of ideas, higher reason, and the idea of good.

Plato says to you: "I love the fact that I am still famous. I have learned and grown since I was on the Earth and have had many lifetimes since the one where I was known as 'Plato.' I have returned to the Earth-school because I wanted to express and expand. This modern world would be very difficult for me to understand. The 'Plato' lifetime was when I was able to pull it all together. I was able to pull the physical, and mental energy together to come up with a great body of work. This was a high point lifetime. There were some mundane lifetimes in spiritual studies. Once, I was a walk-in in North America in the 1800s to help a distraught young woman. It was very interesting to experience her life and to gain an understanding of all the different amenities of the time."

Anwar Sadat—1918-1981

Anwar Sadat was one of thirteen children and born forty

miles North of Cairo in the Nile River delta. He went to both Muslim and Christian schools as a boy. In 1936, military schools were open to lower middle class youths. Much of his youth was spent in actions against the British and other Western influences in Egypt. Sadat always moved in political and military circles. In 1969, he became the Vice President of Egypt under Nasser, and president after Nasser's death in 1970. His battles were over the Suez Canal and with Israel and Palestine. His goals were economic liberalization, an open door economy, and peace with Israel. Sadat and Prime Minister Menachem Begin shared the 1978 Nobel Peace Prize for the Israeli-Egyptian Peace Treaty.

Sadat's open door brought in foreign banks, tourism, and luxury imports. Egyptians made fortunes in oil rich areas but didn't invest in productive industries. Groups became opposed in the 1970s to the Westernization and corruption in everyday Egyptian life. There were internal revolutions and opposition to the peace treaty. Muslim religious radicals shot and killed Anwar Sadat on October 6, 1981, as he was reviewing a military parade.

He says to you: "I have been Home for a while now and am absolutely joy-filled! I am joyful that I was a peacemaker and could see clearly that there needed to be peace in the Middle East. I want you to know that I still work for peace from here. It is my greatest desire to bring peace to Egypt, Israel, and the region. I had many lives in this area of the world and have loved its people and culture and rituals. I love the people still. I have lived many lifetimes all over the region as far back as an Egyptian pharaoh, in which I didn't do very well.

"My interest has always been to put my energy into this area. When I saw what was happening from Home, I took the first opportunity that would work for me to come forward in body form. I want you to know that I loved this lifetime. I was glad I was able to achieve even though I had to worry about my health this lifetime. I didn't know about the assassination, which was a blessing. It was not in my plan, but I would not have stayed much longer. The assassination did a good deal of good, which is not what the assassin wanted. It focused the country and people who were not supporters, on what I had lived for and a new leader."

Louisa May Alcott—1832-1888

Louisa May Alcott was an author of stories for children. She was born in Germantown, Pennsylvania, and lived in Boston and Concord, Massachusetts. She was taught by her father and worked at teaching, sewing, acting, and being a household servant before she found her calling as a writer. She was a nurse during the Civil War. In her writing, she was known for her cheerful, sturdy characters and for her realistic American scenes. *Little Women* of 1867 is her most famous book. Three movies have been made of *Little Women*.

She says to you: "I have learned that I was, in ancient times, a story teller at a King's court. It was too expensive then to use paper to record stories. This life, I had a great urge to create and write and be independent. This was very difficult in the time I lived, but I was determined to write and be published. My reason to come to the Earth was to be a writer.

"I sheltered my privacy in this life. Friends and family did not approve of my goals. This wasn't a typical path for young women in the 1800s even though I had freethinking parents. But, I was determined.

"My book, *Little Women*, was published despite the fact that a woman was the author. It became beloved by many young girls growing up. I have been surprised here to know that it is yet being repeated in movies. There is no ego here at Home, but I am grateful that this has happened. It is good to create something and have it last. *Little Women* was not a biography. There was a lot more to my life than was in this book. A writer takes from what they know. It is not a factual account of my life.

"I want to tell people not to give up no matter what your situation. Even if your dreams seem blighted, there is always help. It may take a different turn but it will work, even when you think it can't happen. I am the perfect example that it can."

Mao Zedong—1893-1976

Mao Zedong was born in Hunan, China, on December 26, 1893. In six years of schooling, Mao developed his own unique writing style and a good understanding of social problems, Chinese history, and current affairs. Early in life, his goal was to help enrich his country. Mao helped reshape the social and political structures of his ancient and populous country. He was dedicated to fight against inequality and injustice. Through much cultural change and revolutions, he often became ruthless. Mao studied Marx, Lenin, Confucius, and Western ways and decided on Communism.

Mao taught school, edited radical magazines, organized trade unions, and began political schools. He was one of the original fifty founders of the Chinese communist party in 1921. He was a key figure in China in the twentieth century and an important reformer. He devoted his life to the advancement of the peasant class, which was terrorized for centuries by those in power. However, in pursuit of his own goals, Mao could be violent and dictatorial. He developed the strategy of encircling the cities from the countryside, mass political thought, and made a bridge between the leaders and the led. He died September 1976, a short time after opening contact with the United States.

The Guides say: "In his defense, it would have been difficult to become the leader of China without using some of the tactics he did. Because he was an evolved soul he was able to take control of the country."

He says to you: "I had the idea that for China to join the modern world that it had to be held in total control. I had a mistaken idea and many lives were lost. I believed that the government had to rule with an iron fist for the people to understand and to work together. I am trying to justify my actions. Are the people not better off under the rule of communism than under the emperors before? There was an improvement in the life of the average Chinese when I came and distributed goods. But China is too big and I needed many subordinates. They became greedy.

"China was not a country of God. I didn't believe in God and was totally surprised when I got Home and saw the truth. Even though I am an evolved soul and have much Earth experience, from a very young age, I didn't believe in the truth of the energy of God. My plan, being born into China, was to help this country. Unfortunately, I did it in a very hard-handed way. To some extent, I was able to make life better for the average Chinese. China is still a country of much repression and hardship. It is difficult to watch some of my ideas being twisted and misused."

Chapter 22

Vacation is Over, Time to go Home

To die is to regroup, relax and review. An interview with a soul leaving Earth to head Home could sound like this . . .

Angel: "How has your holiday been?"

Soul: "Just wonderful. I've seen and done a lot. I've met so many nice people."

Angel: "Well, it's been so nice to have you here. I hope you come again."

Soul: "Thank you. It took me until the last of the trip to really know my way around."

Angel: "Isn't that always the way?"

Soul: "Next trip time, I'll just visit a flatter terrain. The hills here have been so difficult to navigate. It rains a lot here, too."

Angel: "Well, next vacation, choose East of here. Living is a bit easier at the beach, lots of sun. But every holiday has its quirks."

Soul: "That's the truth. The accommodations have been great, but the group I'm traveling with has some real oddballs in it. I've had to learn to tolerate them."

Angel: "Well, that is a good way to handle them. Different people, places, languages, foods, area, are all educational and challenging. We are just glad you chose this spot on Earth to visit."

Soul: "Yeah, at first, I had trouble with the customs here. It took some time to figure out the money exchange and the language. But, I've managed to climb the mountains and be patient with myself in learning new skills. I think I will go to the beach next trip. I'd like to learn to swim."

Angel: "When you do, watch out for hurricanes and sharks."

Soul: "I will. I'll read up on the area first, and choose some teachers, guides, and helpers to make this trip more successful."

Angel: "You seem pretty pleased with yourself. What's in your souvenir bag?"

Soul: "I took rolls and rolls of photos and many videos, so I can remember my experiences here. In this box is patience. Here, wrapped in this plastic bag, is harmony and balance. These took time to find and a lot of energy to purchase. But I did it. Some people found them right away, but I had to look and look for them."

Angel: "Is that a bag of beauty and self-love I see there?"

Soul: "Yes! And what a treasure to get."

Angel: "So I've heard. People are always looking for it to take Home with them. Were you able to get everything you wanted?"

Soul: "Oh, I wish. No. As hard as I tried, I couldn't find forgiveness and real, genuine appreciation. Perhaps on another trip."

Angel: "Well, I wish you the best. Are you all packed and ready to go?"

Soul: "Yes. I can't wait to get Home, unpack, rest up, and be where I am most happy and comfortable.

Everyone will love hearing about my trip. I will miss everyone here, but it's time to go. I've stayed the time I had planned."

Angel: "Well, it was nice having you in our city. Have a safe trip now. Please recommend us to others and come back when you wish."

Soul: "I will. Many thanks for your advice, maps, and suggestions. Be sure to stop and see me at my home, when you're in the area. You know you're always welcome."

Every minute of every day, you are thinking, acting, doing, and creating—maybe in small ways, maybe in big ways. It doesn't matter. You are about your choices and plans as you designed. Just as you planned your lifetime itinerary on the Earth-school, your body design, and your experiences, you also chose the time you would return Home.

Even if you are not aware of it in your thinking mind, your soul beat knows its source of energy and remembers when it is time to flow out and on. On Earth, you call it death. The end. It is only the end of the body, and the time period for which you designed it. As every life and birth on Earth is unique to each soul, so is leaving the body and going Home.

Just before you are born on Earth, is called the "transition" stage. Once again, when you move your energy to leave the body, you are making your transition to your energy source— God, Heaven, or Home.

When you put your energy into the little baby body, you confined your soul in matter and physical boundaries. You had to get used to it, little by little. Now, when your trip is done, little by little, you release the physical, heavy world, so you can fly, soar, and be free flowing and glowing. It is the natural design and plan that you and the All created.

Everyone does not just lie down and pass away to Home. Some do, but there are many ways to cause the soul to leave the body—disasters, accidents, disease, violence, another's freewill interfering with yours, perhaps a drunk driver. One can't really know another's script.

Every soul also has a right to alter their script at any time. The person who pulled through some horrible body damage may have planned to experience this, or decided not to have it be the experience that released their soul.

Since everyone appreciates the energy force it takes to create a physical life form, it is devastating to the mind and emotions when another goes Home. It doesn't matter the physical age. If all souls remembered that Home is the best place to be, and that a life plan has been completed, then the grief would turn to a celebration to cheer the loved soul Home and implore them to wait for you.

Mentally, many people, more and more, know this deeply, somewhere in their minds. Some funeral ceremonies accentuate the celebration of the life finished and Home at last. The physical body has emotions as part of its makeup. And even when the deep belief of everlasting life is realized and understood, the mind and heart still suffer and hurt at the separation. Those who are loved, are deeply missed, because the direct energy of love they gave is temporarily gone. It seems like forever, but it isn't. Even the very old bodies don't get used to all their pals leaving.

The knowledge of life after life and the understanding of the privilege of sharing a life with others, helps the pain that deepens the sad emotions. Sometimes, some beg, "Don't go. Don't leave me." We want what is comfortable and dear to stay with us. It is easier for us to go, than to release another. But, once again, one must pull on the energy of love and say, "If this were me, would I want another to hold me back? To keep me here?" This is especially if the life path is completed. Of course, only the soul leaving knows this for sure, so society decides not to guess and attempts to preserve life. This, too, can get out of hand. Technology interferes too often and won't let go. It is a difficult call. All must learn to trust in their higher good and intuition to guide them. Some souls linger a long time for their own reasons. They may be waiting until loved ones get used to the idea. They may be afraid of what's next. They may be sacrificing a time period so others have the opportunity to care for them and serve them, even work off some karma or allow another to work off karma due them.

The scenarios go on and on. Each soul involved lives the moments and directs the steps. Souls that end their own lives are not in balance. Their choice is devastating and deeply agonizing for loved ones. They will live again, and gain balance in the physical world. They will learn, in time, to love themselves.

To deliberately end another's life breaks the universal rule of not harming any other person. A person murdered will live again, and be repaid for the murderer's misuse. The murderer will study and learn to appreciate life and will repay the debt due.

The most difficult Earth ending is when babies, toddlers, children, and the young, leave those who have shared their brief lives. When the Earth years have been long, it is said, "Oh well, they had a long, full life." But the human mind and heart is squeezed and rattled when a soul that is becoming decides to leave—or is rushed Home through some event. The mind goes blank, the heart is shocked, the soul questions over and over again. Was it this new-soul-on-Earth's plan? If so, why? Or was this young one's life path cut short? And why?

When you and your child-love are together again, they will tell you. The very hard part is stepping into each day after, with a rich memory. In time, give another that love, so that they may thrive in it. Your dharma will double and the soul who went Home will smile and sparkle.

A lot of the grief comes from thinking that the young one had not yet begun to really live. This is your perspective. You do not know what soul growth was achieved and experienced in their brief life. Whatever it was, they chose you to advance and share it. Another day, not far away, your loving souls will blend again.

Some dear souls need help separating their energy from the body. An example is one who had to fight very hard and long to stay alive on Earth to fulfill their plan. It is like holding onto something in your hand really tight. When it is time to let it go, the fingers won't flex and open, because they've gripped tightly a long time.

When you leave Home for Earth or elsewhere, the souls there do not mourn your passing onto another experience. At Home, one can see a bigger picture. They help you pack, make sure you've got your script and maps, and all the energy you need to enjoy the trip. They ask, "Who will take you in? Who will love you and help you?" Then they throw you a Bon Voyage party, toast your crossing and choices, make sure you have your ticket Home, and kiss you good-bye! You're off on an adventure, a vacation. You are giving yourself the opportunity to brighten your soul and make things right. You have an infinite phone credit card to call Home at any time for love and encouragement. And at the minimum, you chose two physically invisible buddies to come along—a physical world guide and an Angel. Good idea. Why not? It's your life, you can do as you can create, but all responsibilities are known.

Souls on Earth and at Home both speak and sing sweetly to help this soul let go. Just as old friends on Earth visits may say,

"It's okay now, you can go. I'll be all right." Soul friends in Heaven visit in dreams and say, "I've missed you. When will you arrive? All is ready for you. You are done." What the soul needs, the soul will have. What the person's belief is, the path and welcoming committee will be ready. All are one and all strive for comfort for all. Fear of dying can be a block to releasing. No one at Home gets tired and there is no time. Each soul is as precious as the next. Always.

Energy lessens as the trip comes to a close. This is like running low on money to do more sightseeing and eating out. You have to get Home and recharge, even go back to classes at Home, if you have forgotten too much. Free tuition. Free everything. In your script, you only brought so much energy with you for the Earth life experience. You left the rest in your bank at Home. If some souls who plan to leave early change their script and stay longer, they often have a tough time. Maybe more struggle in life. It is like one saying, "Well, I don't want to go Home. Yet, I don't have the money (energy) to stay. So, I'll get a job here to rebuild my energy account." The job could be to do good works and get positive energy input from others. Or making that long distance phone call and asking for Mom, Dad, or Home to send more money (energy). It's your call.

You may choose a heart attack, stroke, accident, war, AIDS, cancer, etc. to slow the physical body, to break it down, so you can release your essence, your soul, to go Home. Every day of your Earth lifetime, you have gone up and down your extension cord, plugged into the All energy source. When you sleep, you go Home to visit and re-energize. You reawaken in your body, ready to go and enjoy your life plan. But in all these times, you do not cut the connection or pull the plug. You just flow back and forth. It is most like a light beam.

As people approach ripe older ages, they are drawn to the core of their beginnings. They may become more spiritual.

They may visit childhood homes, look up friends, apologize, contemplate, or sleep more. They may seek out people to right mistakes or relationships, to seek forgiveness or give forgiveness. Their higher self and helpers are aiding them to finish up and put their Earthly life in order. You don't want to leave a mess for another to clean up. And some, if they have not forgotten, remember Home and are preparing for the trip. Whether it is slow or quick, each cell in the body releases its energy to the light beam. When the soul is ready, this happens quickly.

Some souls are very intuitive and know when they have completed all they planned. They can be walking and talking or dancing or sleeping, and zap, they can be Home. They set it up that way. Some souls that linger long are helped by Angels who come to help lovingly rock the body and release the energy. Usually, the life energy departs from the top of the head. There is a snap and pause, and floating and lifting slowly. You have chosen the ending to this life story. If you wish the path to Home to be a rocket, a tunnel, a lightening bolt, a staircase, a flight on eagle's or Angel's wings, it will be as you wish.

It is important to drop the heavy physical matter, as your mind remembers, and allow yourself the freedom to leave Earth behind. Some are so attached to a lifetime, a person, or a place, that they do not accept the demise of their body, and cling to the familiar Earth. This is sad, as there is nothing more they can do. If you know of an Earthbound spirit, a ghost, speak to them lovingly and send them Home. The light is on for them. Souls at Home never give up on trying to pull them Home. It is best, so they can rest and begin again.

As you leave and are glowing all excited, everyone else is crying and holding onto you. Pure love gives freedom. Now is a rest time and healing time for everyone. You do not arrive in limbo or purgatory or any other way station. If you expect

Allah, St. Peter, Angels, The Pearly Gates, Saints, God, Jesus, remember you will be welcomed by whoever makes you feel most comfortable. It is their service to souls that are a part of them. There are souls at Home who specialize in this service. Some are "experts" with soldiers, some with babies and children, some with the very aged. If you need it, it is there. Even the nastiest, most evil, destructive souls that die, are welcomed Home by loved ones. It may take these souls eons of time to evolve and recognize their misuse. Hopefully, this transition begins with loved ones and Angels giving welcoming comfort.

As you are meeting old friends at Home who came there before you from this lifetime and others, your loves still on Earth are focusing in ceremonies on getting used to the idea of letting you go. You may even visit your funeral. This is why it is said, "Don't speak ill of the dead." They can hear you and see you. Not always, but sometimes, as the soul desires. Those left on Earth pray and support one another. They express love and relive your life in memories. Each life is a story from which to learn. All the good is expressed to the next soul and so on, to help them.

"Help them do what?" you may ask. Help them to recognize that they are one with the All. That one is not complete without this consciousness of all the others. If one flower is beautiful, then a bouquet is more beautiful. The more souls in recognition of one mind, one source, the smoother, the easier, the more flowing and brighter our light. So many souls linger in despair and shadows. One's strength gives another strength to serve the parts of you that don't choose well.

The journey Home is quick, and soon becomes familiar. There is no fear, but music, and sights of beauty and peace. You are pure thought, pure light, and are free. To Home you go, to waiting, loving arms. It is a short trip, but traumatic. A spot is ready for you where you can sleep and rest a while from "jet lag." Later, you awaken, visit others, and go back and rest. You take your time, as there is none and no urgency, to get used to Home. In time, you may take a tour, look up old friends, or you may sit, observe, and think. When a passing has been very quick or involved a long illness, often, souls, though knowing it is done, need to release the mind and emotion of the memory. There also could have been great fear before passing and not of the soul's choice of time. Souls rest and loved ones visit to whisper loving thoughts of comfort. They offer you little remembrances of Home. Patience and love is endless.

Every living thing is part of the energy of the All and you and I. Some living things have more energy depending on their choice of the experience they want. Animals and plants for instance are beautiful sparks of energy that evolved souls created to serve on the Earth. Plant energies give us food, beauty, and benefit the planet's circulation of oxygen. Animals are here for beauty as well, and some also serve as food for man.

Like all other energies that visit the Earth, plants and animals have a time frame in which they will be born, then live, serve, and die. Plant energy returns Home when finished just as man and animal energies return home. There is a place at Home for all energies when they choose to rest, learn, change, and sometimes evolve. When beloved pets die, who have entertained, been companions, and were loved as family members, their soul energy returns to rest before reawakening to take on another service.

When there are human beings who suffered great trauma in life, perhaps were mentally ill and confused, or took their own life, it usually takes a long time for their experiences to be sorted out and for them to awaken and understand that they are Home and what has occurred. In these situations, often a pet energy such as that of a dog, cat, bird, or some other gentle creature will accompany these souls. They will sit by and wait—their energy is of comfort. They are unconditionally loving companions to a resting soul, just as they were on Earth.

Sometimes, animals from past lifetimes will be present to greet a returning soul to provide comfort and familiarity while a soul adjusts to Home. Once again, there is no division—everyone goes Home to the same place and one must treat all energies lovingly. Pets are protectors, teachers, confidantes, and friends. They are to be treated with the same degree of kindness one would offer a human friend. They take joy in your life as you do in theirs.

REMEMBER . . .

- To die is to relax, regroup, and review your energies.
- Did your Earth experience go well?
- There are many ways to die but the destination is the same for everyone—Home.
- Being left behind hurts.
- Suicide is an unbalanced act.
- Babies that go Home teach tough lessons.
- What the soul needs is what the soul will have at Home.
- Even the evil are welcomed Home.
- Loved pets serve at Home as well as here.

Chapter 23

The Future and Beyond

Take heart, Dear Ones. As you have been a part of the creation of all that has come to pass, so you will be a part of all that is to come. The most recent ages have been the Industrial Age, to a time now, that most call the Information Age. In the last hundred years, man's manipulation and creative use of energy has leaped from horseback to space stations. An idea once took decades to travel to other areas of the Earth. Now, an idea, in full living color with sound effects, can be zapped around the world in seconds. Mental hospitals have been emptied due to a new understanding and new medicines to help those in emotional pain. Medicines and cures have gone from back woods crude to magnetic and laser wonderment. The body machine we designed is better-understood every day.

As always, however, and as needs be, there will exist all levels for learning and growth on the Earth-school planet. What your grandparents couldn't have imagined has come to be in everyday use. And what you can't dream up today, in the future, will be smarter, better, modern, advanced, scientific, and new. Everyone's ideas build upon one another's and flow into becoming realities—hopefully, useful and positive realities. The next age to unfold is the age of oneness and tolerance. Little by little and step by step, mankind will learn, understand, and practice a unity among all.

Souls come and go every day to the Earth. Finished souls go Home with old ideas and return, in time, with new ones to build upon. They repair the mistakes in old thinking and replace them with new and better ways of thinking. This takes the coming and going of many masses of soul energy since each grows at one's own pace. The planet Earth is a big, living, breathing energy. Mankind has not cared well for its home Earth. Everything men and women do on the planet affects its evolvement. Earth is a mass of energy and is evolving, too.

A great physical upheaval may be necessary to cleanse the planet from damage and the poison of too many toxins. This will enable the Earth to right itself and its inhabitants to gain a complete understanding of Earth as a living organism, and man's role in oneness with it. This cleansing will slow technology and new creations, as men and women will be totally occupied with working together to rebuild and recreate. What better way than through a worldwide clean up and building project is there to really look and see and communicate with your fellow men and women?

Man will be thrown backwards in how he lives for a while. Many souls will go Home and many once populated areas will be gone. It may take as much as twenty years for things to move forward again as the know-how of technology is in people's minds. For souls gone Home, this time will serve as an opportunity to observe, catch up, and learn. It will be a time of harmony and joy to all and will be observed by all at Home.

From these days on, every soul on Earth and those coming to Earth will have the first and foremost thought of not making a move without considering how their actions could harm the planet. Just as the seed of thought was carried from Home to Earth of "A Messiah is coming," a seed of thought of "Protect the planet" will be foremost in everyone's minds. Many new advances will come about with this new way of thinking. Some ideas won't be permitted because of harm to the Earth. Fossil fuels won't be used. The advancement of technology will progress at a slower pace due to some technology not being Earth-friendly.

Once a forward movement begins, life improvements will move at a rapid pace as there will be fewer people and they'll have new ideas—act like a committee all of one mind on a project in which they don't have to sort through material, argue, and convince others of the best way to do something. Also, by the time this clean up occurs, there should be a better understanding by men and women of how to use their energies, remember who they are, why they are here, and how to be aware of their spiritual guides. With purer energies after the cleansing, the spirit guides can move closer to the Earth to work with mankind.

Before these days, however, there will be more great spiritual leaders, teachers, and examples. Remember, your awareness of who you are, and how your energy affects others and the whole galaxy, is the Second Coming! No one anywhere is ruling you! It is a popular idea that "a God" or some other entity causes this or that to happen. It is a trait of humankind to want to have someone or something to blame. This takes away the individual's responsibility for his choices. Eventually, this belief will pass away as it dawns on most that we are one energy. Fortunately, the word is out and many know this already and are spreading it around. It will be contagious. It is truth. When teachers arrive, pay attention. They have just come to help remind you of who you are.

There is nothing to fear in the future. Whatever you face and experience, remember, it is an opportunity that you set up to do better. If you are Home, you will continue to learn and be with loved ones and may observe all new creations and changes on Earth. If you are on the planet, you will be protecting it fiercely while rebuilding slowly in new and improved ways.

This is to come about in the next hundred years if energies that promote awareness, self-love, unconditional love, tolerance, understanding, and respect for others are picked up and carried on. It is well under way with more openness and expression among people. People are also realizing that there is more than their physical self and physical world. And then there are billions upon trillions of choices to be made to get us all there.

In these days ahead, people will learn to be better to one another. It will be a planet of more cooperation, less prejudice, and less violence. It is hoped that violence won't be a form of entertainment as it is now. More evolved souls will be born on the Earth than young souls. Older souls are not as keyed into the density of the physical body and the senses as young souls are. With more understanding, it will be easier to move forward and technology will connect everyone on the planet even more. Teams of people of like minds will look at Earth as a living being that needs to be protected. There will be greater acceptance of blended races and a better system for those who break the rules. A beautiful aspect of this time is that we will bring the idea from Home that life is joyous. And we will remember Home.

In the nearer future, laying groundwork for the far out future, there will be more laws made "with teeth" to allow older people to stay in the work force. Because of the "run-for-the-money" and the influence of mass media, older people are not revered. People are brainwashed that only young and beautiful is worthwhile. This is not a universal truth. Nor is it that only certain body types are attractive or unattractive. There will be a shift in thinking more about the soul within the created body. Older entertainers will start new careers on television and in films that will influence a more positive outlook on aging. The United States will no longer have a "silent majority." Baby steps will be taken every day by people in realizing who they are and in speaking up for themselves and others. As one learns who they are, they treat others better and are treated better.

Television is not now going in the direction it should be going at this time. People are using TV as a directional tool and it is short-circuiting their lives. They believe that television shows them how to live their lives. Sex is about bonding and intimacy, not to sell things. Sex is often used to fill an emptiness of not knowing who you are. A spiritual point of view is missing. Sex is seen as a normal part of life in most countries other than the United States. Thanks to a race consciousness from the Puritan founders, this idea has not yet been transformed. Sex becomes a focal point and of extreme interest. People believe sex can give one power, comfort, and importance. Television shows promote this and the media focuses on it to sell products. It is an unrealistic viewpoint with expectations that won't be satisfied. It is an area that has a lot of room for improvement. Fortunately, there are some positive life models to teach and entertain.

Fidel Castro bolsters up Cuba on his charisma. But life is very difficult in Cuba. When Castro goes Home, a lock against freedom will be gone and a young generation will promote a shifting of ideas. With a new leader, embargoes can be lifted and the people of Cuba can join the new thoughts of the world. The child, Elian Gonzales, won't forget what he saw in Florida. He now knows of a different life. His time in Florida was a good experience even though he needed to be with his father. In time, when he chooses, Elian Gonzales will be a leader in Cuba.

It will be a long while until there is change in the Middle East's drastic warring. Great leaders have tried to stop the fighting. This is a hot spot every day on the planet. It is unbelievable and heart wrenching. Every day, we here at Home send hope and love to those who work for ideas of peace. This area is an example of very young souls totally caught up in emotions and losing control of them. One would think that some would look around the world and say, "Why are we living like this?"

But this idea can't happen because emotions are valued more than logical outcomes. When a mother raises a son telling him he is a hero if he dies fighting, it is difficult to change this belief. These souls, caught up in their emotions, get a high from running through the streets yelling, shooting, and throwing stones. They enjoy it. It is their daily life.

There are evolved souls helping and working with positive energy to make peace but in a region where there has never been peace, it is difficult for people to understand it. The Palestinians and Israelis both have rights on their sides, but it is difficult to get them to sit down and be calm and logical. Pray for them. They are your fellow men and women. A lot of loving energy needs to go there in hopes that there will be some intellectual movement and not just emotional.

The future is full of wonderful living and creating experiences. Remember that Earth is not the only planet. There are many galaxies to explore and other places to live. Some are nothing like Earth. Nor are the physical bodies on them. It depends on what you design in using your free will and what your soul wants to experience. There is a planet that has little land mass and is mostly water. There is also a place where there are more choices of body forms than male and female— but they have their problems, too. A new planet in another galaxy is being established that is physically similar to Earth. The skies are not quite the same color and its three suns are its energy source. It has the same atmosphere as Earth, so the chosen body form is like that of Earthlings. Earth, being the favorite planet of soul travel, is overpopulated and continues to want to be this way. There are some very old soul volunteer pioneers that took refined body forms, so there was no need to start over with body evolvement since it's already been done. These pioneer souls know who they are and mentally keep in touch with Home. Once in matter form, they have to deal with moving matter around and everything has to be created from scratch. From Home, it is very interesting and exciting to watch. Maybe one day this will be your planet of choice.

Another example of a life style you are familiar with from science fiction books, movies, and UFO descriptions, are the beings often portrayed with the little bodies and very large eyes. These beings are very intellectual and have made many discoveries on how to use and be part of the Universe without misusing it. To be scientific is prized in their society. They do not have the health problems Earthlings have and are more evolved. They understand the rules of the Universe and how to move through it and to other solar systems. They are better now at visiting other planets and putting energies in place so that they are not seen and, if they are seen that it is forgotten. They, too, are a part of the All and haven't the right to harm or interfere with other being's lives. They learn through traveling and visiting other places. In the past, they have made mistakes. They are learning as you are. However, their problem is learning how to integrate an emotional part into their intelligence. This is their lesson and what they are learning. All souls need to be well-rounded to move forward. In order for them to experience spirit fully and have total memory, they must use emotions as well as intelligence. Emotions are needed to gain understanding and to use the love that the Universe is. Emotions are the connectedness and feeling of love needed to be expressed on canvas, in music, or in a book, which draws people together. It is most difficult for the musicians and artists of this other society because many of their fellow souls do not understand how vital the emotions are.

Perhaps you know a very intellectual person that doesn't seem to grasp his or her emotions and expression of love. Maybe they came from this planet in a previous lifetime where the intellect was very well understood and emotions were not.

To have one and not the other leaves a soul lacking. Maybe they are here to learn and have a more well-rounded experience. Our brothers and sisters in the Middle East are caught up in all emotion and very little intellect to be balanced. They, too, are lacking. Some intellectuals think they don't want to "stoop" to an emotional level. This is because the emotions are difficult to deal with.

The extraterrestrials may be healthier, as they do have different bodies than Earthlings, but thoughts cause illness, just as emotions or lack of expressing them can. To know about these other life societies helps to understand one another better. For many years, people on Earth have had, in stories and pictures, glimpses of these different people. The people who write about them or create films and books about them could have been a part of this society at one time and are remembering. Or, people know how to tap into the universal consciousness, which is a constant flow of information available whenever any soul is ready to receive knowledge. This may be similar to an experience all souls have, when they come to a realization, suddenly understanding something new. Today, this is, in fun, called the "ah ha" moment! Many creative people are tapped into this "library" and can churn out ideas and innovations daily. It is available to everyone.

We Angels are all learning, as are the water beings, you on Earth, the old souls on the new planet, and the souls choosing one of the multi-body forms. It is all about experience. Perhaps your future will be involved in one of these experiences. Maybe, in your next life, you will choose to go to another galaxy and create another body form in which to express yourself. Or, maybe you will stay Home and rest and play and travel. You may teach others, or be taught. There's no rush. There's no time.

Whoever you are, and whatever you do, you are not alone.

Every soul is striving through their life experiences wherever they are. Be joyful in your creative freedom. Embrace the beauty of your energy that is you. Love it and don't be afraid to leap for love and all possibilities.

REMEMBER . . .

- Earth souls have learned a lot in a short time.
- Ideas come and go as souls come and go.
- First priority—protect the planet.
- Planetary clean up is coming.
- Committees on the same page of ideas get things done faster and better.
- A further blending of races and ideas ahead.
- Teachers are coming to help.
- There is nothing to fear.
- Home will be remembered.
- The aged will be more revered.
- Friends from other galaxies learn from us.
- A new planet is being prepared.

Chapter 24

Whatever You Do . . .

The most important words are Change, Choice, Love, One, Tolerance, and Forgive. My Dears, who are one with me, say the following aloud and believe it. It is truth.

1. I am perfect.
2. I can do anything.
3. I can change everything.
4. I am a part of All energy forces, everywhere.
5. Without me, these forces are not complete.
6. Where and who I am now, I designed and planned.
7. I am enjoying the eternal, universal flow.
8. I have all the time I need to become all I desire.
9. I am a unique, glorious being, a part of every aspect of all creation.
10. I can never die.
11. I am love.
12. My thoughts, words, and deeds are divinely creative.
13. I meet all men and women in a place called tolerance.
14. They are me. I am them. We are one.
15. My energy is gold and I use it well.
16. I have every chance I need to make my choices.
17. I see my sparkling soul, my fine physical being, and God in the mirror.
18. I am great, good, glorious, wonderful, and joyous.
19. I am divinely, infinitely, inexhaustibly, perpetually loving.

Read these thoughts often, as it is so very important that you know how special, beautiful, and loved you are. If ever you are in doubt, lift up in your mind and think of me, your Angel. I will be with you before your thought is done. Picture my wings around you, and diamonds spread at your feet to guide your steps. We are an unbeatable team, you and I.

All I have written to you on these pages, you already know. You have just forgotten Home. Like grandparents or parents telling you what you were like when you were little, I wish you to remember and understand who you are and your mission on your Earth vacation.

Have a wonderful time in your life on Earth. Bring Home lots of souvenirs (lessons learned). I am with you every day. I will be with you on the ride Home. Together, we will join the welcoming committee, as hugs and applause are lavished upon you.

I am so honored to be your chosen helper. Do your best now. Until you can "see" me again, think on these things and whatever you do, do it lovingly.

Your Angel

To be continued, as you will continue, without end.

Say What?
A Glossary of Terms

Akashic Records: The video tape (or CD) of all your lifetime experiences. This can be viewed by you at Home to review your uses of energy through all of time. Or, access can be gained through a Guide in service. One must have permission to view another's tape. Your tapes are off limits to others upon your request. (Just think it.)

Angels: Energy beings that have chosen not to put their energy in a physical form on Earth or other galaxy places. They chose to learn through serving their fellow men and women invisibly.

Anti-Christ: Those who, for their own gain, would misuse positive energy to influence many souls and test them. An energy stuck in a negative way of thinking and being.

Buddha: A person who has achieved enlightenment.

Birth: New. To begin in a new place of one's soul's choice. On Earth: To put one's energy in a contained space for a chosen length of time to experience a chosen path for the balancing of energy and for soul growth.

Christ: Anointed one, a teacher. A good example, a focus of positive use of energy and the laws of energy: Created good draws more creative good.

Death: A term for the release of the soul from the physical body the soul created. To pass over. Transition. Bite the dust. Kick the bucket. Breakdown of the physical body designed for one lifetime. Born again at Home. Not an ending. A celebration since everyone wants to GO HOME after a day's (lifetime) experience. A new beginning without the burden of matter and time. A change in location of action. Once occurring, a free flowing energy in total freedom and a Universe of love.

Devil: A negative use of positive energy. Causing harm that will have to be corrected later. If not in this lifetime, in another. The devil: one who chooses to be rotten and mean and nasty. A real troublemaker.

Dharma: Positive energy created when one creates loving, giving, caring situations towards one's self and their fellow men and women and situations. Can be drawn on like a "bonus" in a lifetime.

Disease: The interruption of flowing, positive energy. Often created by allowing negative energy into the body. Often designed by the soul to experience for their own reasons. Can be a sacrificial choice to teach others (family, caregivers).

Dream: What can occur when the body is recharging at Home. Loved ones and guides may try to send you information in dream form. Your higher self may be advising, warning you in picture form. Your "joy" guide may be entertaining you. Your mind may be stressed and things are being resolved, worked out, and reorganized in your dream time. A teaching/learning tool to help you in your Earth-school experience.

Earth: A school planet you helped design to enjoy, play, and create on. A masterful design of great beauty. A home away from home for a little while. Used to perfect one's soul growth.

Ethers: The air, vibrations of flowing air. Unseen but dynamic carrier of thoughts to all corners of the galaxy.

Evil: A temporary condition of heavy-duty negative, nasty use of energy. All negative energy can be transformed to positive energy (think about it).

Fear: A mental thought that stops creativity. Another word for halt. Causes blockage of energy flowing freely for positive use.

Forgiveness: A healing use of energy that recognizes the struggle of negative energy to be transformed to positive energy. The removal of negative energy from another (or situation) so one can flow and become better. To not forgive is like keeping the pain and hurt after being cured from a terminal illness.

Fortune Teller—Psychic—Prophet: All the same. *Everyone* is "psychic." Meaning, "knows things." You have been around, many, many times. Your experience and knowledge is vast. You may have chosen *not* to remember it all *now*.

No soul can predict the future energies, because millions and millions of souls are making choices every second. So how these choices fall into place and become, is very difficult to see.

However, an energy (above listed) may see a number of possibilities that could happen. The prophet has a huge responsibility not to influence or interfere with choices. Serious karmic debt can be racked up to do so.

Free Will—Choice: All yours to do with as you wish in thoughts, words, and actions. The ultimate right of every energy spark. Total freedom to choose your path at Home or on Earth or wherever. Since all energy is good, to misuse it requires "putting it back as you found it" through your freewill or positive choice.

God: Big energy mass of every single soul together. Constantly creating, thinking, being. Never ending. Good energy to use as one wishes.

Group Consciousness: A shared way of thinking by many. Aware of a positive (or negative) way to believe, and behave. All in agreement that this is acceptable.

Example: The group believes smoking is okay. The group believes smoking is horrible.

Group consciousness occurs slowly (in Earth time).

Guide: A teacher. A soul at Home who chose to help one or more individuals or groups on Earth, or other worlds. This is done by sending in thought encouragement, love, and positive energy. A guide cannot interfere with a fellow soul's choice. They stand by, observe, listen, wait, and hope. A guide may be in sync with a physical Earth person, who can "call them up" to come "down" to serve through teaching souls on Earth. The Earth person is the phone operator making the connection.

Hate: Doesn't feel good. A crippling use of positive energy changed to negative energy through thoughts, words, and actions. Must be corrected in time.

Heaven: Home. Where *all* energy resides. All life paths begin and continue here.

Hell: A fictional place of regret, punishment, hot fire, vermin, and pain. A fearful place people are told they will go when they die, if they don't shape up and are good. Does not exist. Fictional.

Karma: Accumulated mistakes. The negative energy that is

created by not loving yourself or your fellow man the very best way. Buy now, pay later. Requires fixing and correcting.

Karmic Debt: A misuse of negative energy that can be fixed by experiencing it oneself and/or making it up to one, or a group that was harmed.

Karmic Illness: A state of imperfection. Cause and effect to satisfy debt. An opportunity one set up for oneself to erase karma and right misuse.

Karmic Mate: Another soul you owe something to. Or, they owe you. You chose to share a lifetime to fix or correct a past misuse of energy.

Lifetime: One of many, many, many thoughts one thinks to design and create, to experience a multitude of situations and personalities. Hence, understanding fellow souls' choices and oneself. A block of time chosen to live in a physical form, or other universal place, to experience creative energy.

Love: The perfect way to express oneself through thoughts, word and action. A positive use of energy. Creates good energy. And, it feels good, too.

Marriage: A man-woman made device to combine energies. An opportunity to share learned experiences, create new ones, and pay up previous debts. A contract, a focus. A pooling of energies for focusing on a goal. Often joined by other energies (see Sex) who want, need to be, experiencing with the married pair. A device to maintain order. Not always for a lifetime. Often, lessons are learned and debt is paid and the contract is over.

Money: A man-made creation of energy to exchange for other energy creations. Can be used to create negative or positive thoughts, actions, and things. Earth-school tool to move energy. It often blocks souls from flowing.

New Age: Every energy, every day, is new. Usually a block of time where the group consciousness raises up a notch in positive thinking. Example: In 1856, slavery is good. In 1995, slavery is horrible.

Prayer: Positive thinking. Mantra. Putting-out-the-thought to the Universe for good energy to transform negative energy.

Religion: The club who thinks the way you do. The group you chose to be in to help you, in your physical lifetime, to use and understand your spiritual self. They help you use your energy positively. A focus to remember who you are.

Sex: An exchange of energy. Should feel good. Can create a third (or more) energy.

Sin: A word to define a misuse of energy. Usually having to be paid for in hell. Comes in degrees of awfulness! (From gossip to murder.)

Soul and Spirit: The spark of you. Perfect, complete energy a part of the All/God energy. Without your soul, the All is not complete. Eternal, never, ever ending.

Soul mate: Another soul that you have spent lifetimes with. One who agreed to "travel" with you again and help and teach you. A buddy or love. Any sex. Sometimes for all of a lifetime and sometimes for a part.

Time: A name for blocks of contained energy. Millennium—1000 years. Eon—gobs of thousands of years. Year—365 days. Months—twelve to a year. Hour—What seems endless when waiting for a lover or to have a baby, or when you are in pain. Lifetime: Your choice of a block of time to travel to Earth to experience creative use of energy. Time: That which does not exist at Home.

Tired: Does not exist at Home/ Heaven! An Earth-school lack of energy. Recharged by sleep. Plugging into the Home energy source to keep the physical body going.

Tolerance: That which takes a leap in consciousness to do and teach by example. The recognition of where one's fellow man is in his life path and not interfering with its flow. Acceptance of differences, just as you want others to mind their own business.

Twin Flame: Your soul, split in half. Each individual, same energy. Responsible for own choices. Doubles creative power (more fun). Either a difficult or wonderful coupling when together on school planet Earth.

Higher Self: The part of your soul that remembers who you are and why you are experiencing what you are. Not influenced by one's personality. Ask from the Higher Self, and you shall receive. Your own private library about you. The *you* that knows best.

Example:

Personality Self—I am so jealous she won the contest.

Higher Self—Good for her! I wish for her (who is part of me) all good fortune.

Life Path: The Earth-school experience the soul designs with others. Who will do what and what can happen. A mission one sets up. A thing of truth and beauty when a life path is fulfilled as one wants.

Levels of Soul Growth

New Soul: All souls are the same age, but, young or old in their creative experiences. A new soul may be one just deciding to create. Or, on the Earth plane, one of little lifetime experiences in physical world living. One that may enter a primitive life form.

Young Soul: We all were young once! The more we do, think, feel, and study, the older we get. A young soul has a good start and all is possible. When one doesn't "get it" and they aren't conscious of some energy uses, we just have to love and encourage them more. You wouldn't ask a baby to fly a plane.

Old Soul: An energy spark that has followed many paths and made many commitments to their soul growth (and others). Once new and once young, now basking in higher understandings of how and why they use their energy (not always consciously). But, the eyes are deep and they reflect a strong center balance.

Lost Soul: No such thing can happen. A soul may linger near the Earth plane after putting the body down. Or, a soul may hover and wait while a walk-in helps complete a path. Or, a soul may astral travel while a body lies in a coma. Or, a soul may wait while a person's mind does not function. A confused person may "seem" lost. All souls are loved and accounted for. None can be lost. A soul that chooses evil or cruel energies to harm others is not lost. Just slowed down. All souls always have every opportunity to choose to right misuse and become brighter, lighter, and triumphant over any past misuses. And being a part of them, we wish right choices for them, too!

Evolved Soul: Used to describe a soul that has grasped, practiced, taught, and been the example of oneness of all life and expresses unconditional love.

Master Soul: A dedicated teacher of the All energies. A specialist in moving about the Universe with perfect understanding of who's who and what's what. Understandably, an old soul. One with vast experience that has been applied to the divine order and love of all beings everywhere.

Lords of Karma: Fancy name, tough job. The guidance counselors on the Universal Travel Web. Those who lovingly serve fellow souls leaving Home and coming Home. The keepers of the records. The lifetime advisors and matchmakers. What place, family, circumstance fits your need for a lifetime experience to give you opportunity for soul growth? They help you think about it. Give you insight, suggestions. The choice is always yours. When Home again, at your request, will review your experiences with you. The Grandparents of the Universe. Loving ideas and perfect understanding of you and your soul.

The Teachers

The Teachers
Those Who Show the Way

These are the well-known teachers of new thoughts in their time. Each has thousands and thousands of disciples to teach their ideas and to serve as examples.

As *you* lead *your* life, others watch and learn.

Moses	1250 BC
Buddha	563 BC
Confucius	551 BC
Jesus	5 AD (approx.)
Mohammed	570 AD
Mohandas Gandhi	1869-1948
Mother Theresa	1910-1997
Pope John Paul II	1920-
Sai Baba	1926-
Martin L. King, Jr.	1929-1968
Dalai Lama	1935-
Diana Spencer	1961-1997

These souls all met (and meet) their fellow men and women on the world stage with unconditional love. They all chose a path of teaching by example and expressed the truth of the oneness of all men and women and the capability for transformation of every soul.

Belief Groups
(not a complete list)

Groups of people who choose to express their spirituality in different beliefs.
There are no chosen people.

Hindu
Jesus Freaks
Bahaism
Assemblies of God
Scientology
Parsiism
Methodists
Unity
Catholic
Lutheran
Taoism
Confucianism
Atheists
Baptists
Judaism
Episcopalian
Buddhist
Muslim
Russian Orthodox
Holy Roller
Revival Ministries

Shakers
Voo Doo
Street Christians
Jainism
Shintoism
Druids
Sikhism
Apostolic
Pentecostal
Gospel Churches
Church of England
Pagans
Deliverance/Christ Churches
Evangelical Protestant
Quakers
Jehovah's Witnesses
Mennonite
Christ Life
Living Word
The Church of Jesus Christ
    of Latter-day Saints
(also known as Mormons)

New Age
Presbyterian
Church of Christ Scientists
Religious Science
Dunkards
Amish
Seventh Day Adventists
Islam
Nazarene
Shamanism

Presbyterian Orthodox
Unitarian
Wesleyan Evangelical
Hari Krishnas
Agnostic
Tribal Worship
New Asian religions
Chinese Folk religions
Spiritism
Jedi Knights

Church of God/In Christ/Prophesy
Anglican Catholic/Bysantine Catholic
Missionary/Worship/Christian Centers
Independent/Fundamental/Freewill
Community/Brethren/Disciples of Christ

The Hardest Things to Do

Admit a wrong

Keep quiet for another's benefit

Release Fear

Wait

Go when it is time

Forgive yourself

Forgive others

Live in the Now

Love unconditionally

Look one you have wronged in the eye

Say you are sorry

Give a speech

Put your elbow in your ear

Spell "Lingerie"

The Most Important Words

Change

Choice

Love

One

Tolerance

Forgive

The Golden Rule

DO UNTO OTHERS, AS YOU WOULD HAVE
THEM DO UNTO YOU.

(Because in the whole scheme of things, what you do to others you do to yourself.)

Love your neighbor as yourself.

I am my brother's keeper.

What you do to others, you do to me.

CHRISTIANITY

All things whatsoever ye would that men should do to you, do ye even so to them.

BUDDHISM

Do not others in ways that you yourself would find hurtful.

JUDAISM

What is hateful to you, do not to your fellow man.

ISLAM

No one of you is a believer until he desires for his brother that which he desires for himself.

CONFUCIANISM

Do not unto others what you would have them not do unto you.

TAOISM

Regard your neighbor's gain as your own gain and your neighbor's loss as your own loss.

THE HIPPOCRATIC OATH

(The physician's oath based on Greek medical thought and ethics.)

. . . If I fulfill this oath and do not violate it, may it be granted to me to enjoy life and art, being honored with fame among all men for all time to come; if I transgress it and swear falsely, may the opposite of all this be my lot.

NATIVE AMERICAN

"The Earth does not belong to us—
We belong to the Earth.
Mankind did not weave the web of life,
We are but one strand in it.
Whatever we do to the web,
We do to ourselves."
1884, Chief Seathl

Guiding Verses— Reminding You to be Good!

You reap what you sow.

What goes around comes around.

An eye for an eye.

You'll get yours, one of these days.

You'll get what's coming to you.

Before you act, think, "Do I want it now or later?"
(the consequences)

You made your bed, now lie in it—then, remake it.

Speak These Truths

I am perfect.

I can do anything.

I can change everything.

I am a part of all energy forces, everywhere.

Without me, these forces are not complete.

Where and who I am now, I designed and planned.

I am enjoying the eternal, universal flow.

I have all the time I need to become all I desire.

I am a unique, glorious being, a part of every aspect of creation.

I can never die.

I am love.

I meet all of mankind in a place called tolerance.

They are me. I am them. We are one.

Our energy is gold and we use it well.

I have every chance I need to make my choices.

I am great, good, glorious, and joyous.

I see my sparkling soul, fine physical being, and God in the mirror.

A Greeting

May the best in me, greet the best in you!

We are one mind, one source, and one destination.

Let the sharing of time and space and experience enhance us both.

May my strengths fill in your gaps and vice versa.

If we are to learn from one another, our energies will work together—maybe bumpy, maybe flowing.

You are amazing, because you are a part of our creation with all our brothers' and sisters' energies!

I praise your choices, your path, your timing, your accomplishments, and hurdles.

There is no division in positive energy.

Greeting Babies and Children

Hello, brave soul.

How dear and adventurous you are to contain your energy in a little body.

I will love you to help you adjust to the Earth-school.

You chose these parents and family and friends.

To begin again is wonderful.

I pray every opportunity you need for your soul growth flows to you.

May your life path be nurtured from here and Home, all the days of your lifetime.

Greeting a Long Time and Aged Friend

Hello my friend.

I honor the long path you've lived.

What can we share and learn from one another?

We have been together a long time.

Have we done what we set out to do?

Thank you for your energy.

Are you ready to go Home?

I'll miss you if you go first.

Leave the light on for me.

I'll be with you soon.

Remember, in eternity, soon is pretty quick!

When You Don't Understand

- Ask: What is going on here?

- Ask: Why am I involved? Do I need to be?

- Ask: What am I learning from this experience?

- Try to be tolerant, if you are not approving, condoning or in agreement.

- Their life path is not your life path.

- People with hard lives are working on karma and are examples for others.

- Be glad you don't need to experience it.

- Try to understand and be kind so that you don't have to experience it.

- Send in thought and love, positive energy to complete their mission.

- Think and hope they do better next time.

Holy Books

Torah—Jewish

Bible—Christian

Dead Sea Scrolls—both Torah and Bible

Koran—Islam

Karmas—
The Energies of the Numbers

1 = Creativity

    Begin, create, start, initiate.

    Can you inspire, lead, and serve in this way?

2 = Patience

    Tolerance, with self and others.

    Can you go with the flow, be helpful, try to understand?

3 = Expression

    Can you say what you want and need to?

    Writing, Art, gardening, music, speaking.

    Much is accomplished by helping others to express themselves.

4 = Work

    Do you put forth the effort to sustain yourself? Get the answers? Supply others' needs?

    A work ethic of getting the job done right, a tenacity to stick to it and complete the task.

    Your work supplies services to others.

    Work physically, mentally, emotionally, spiritually.

5 = Freedom

    Do you want to be free? Need to be?

    Have you kept another from freedom of choice, expression, movement, or thought?

    If you could FLY, would you want to be in a cage?

6 = Responsibility

> Can you take care of yourself? Others?
>
> What you cause, do you take credit for, good or bad?
>
> Can you be an example for others to be committed, loyal, to be counted on?
>
> Do you let others down, or lift them up?
>
> Do you recognize you are one with all mankind and share a group consciousness?
>
> What parts of it are you responsible for?

7 = Spirituality

> Do you remember who you are? Have you faith?
>
> Does your heart and soul know? Are you seeking answers?
>
> Teaching others through example and deeds, the Golden Rule.
>
> Are you a shining soul who is glad to see the best in everyone?

8 = Material Goods

> How do you use, get, and enjoy your stuff? Fairly?
>
> What is the importance of your stuff?
>
> It stays on Earth when you go Home!
>
> It is fun to create and get and have.
>
> Share it all. Be generous.
>
> The more you give, the more you get.
>
> Try it! Let yourself go. Surprise someone.

9 = Finishing—Brotherhood

> Once you have 1-8 down pat, you naturally want to move on.
>
> Example: No need to repeat elementary school once you've done it.
>
> Have you "tested" yourself on all the 1-8 energies?
>
> It may take umpteen lifetimes. That's okay.
>
> Brotherhood is a firm recognition and appreciation for

all energies working together.

On Earth you may finish a job, relationship, illness, project, etc.

Can you move on when it is done?

There is no finish. We keep creating. See #1 above.

Lives in Service and/or Fulfilling Karmic Debt

Here I am. I am a part of you. How will you love the part of you that is me?

Mental illness

Alzheimer's

Down's Syndrome

Autism

Retardation

Cystic Fibrosis

Multiple Sclerosis

Abnormalities

Brief Lives

Those Not Responsible for Debt

Babies

Children

Mentally ill

Mentally deficient

Soldiers at war (in right use)

The Ten Commandments

I.   I am the Lord, thy God, thou shall not have strange gods before me.

II.   Thou shall not take the name of the Lord thy God in vain.

III.   Keep holy the Sabbath Day.

IV.   Honor your Father and your Mother.

V.   Thou shall not kill.

VI.   Thou shall not commit adultery.

VII.   Thou shall not steal.

VIII.   Thou shall not bear false witness against your neighbor.

IX.   Thou shall not covet thy neighbor's wife.

X.   Thou shall not covet thy neighbor's goods.

What We All Have in Common

Need for food, shelter

Male

Female

Laughter

Love

Mother—Father

Music

Math

Crying

Touch

Aging

Birth—Death

Fears

Pain—Physical, Mental, Emotional

To be loved and accepted unconditionally

The desire to be loved by the one you love

Divine Laws

Each is responsible for the misuse of energy

The responsibility is met by repayment

Each has freewill (choice)

The species animal and human will not procreate

Order

Balance of Negative and Positive

Constant change

Law of choice—You get what you ask for, positive or negative

You can have what you want as long it doesn't interfere with someone else's rights

No physical adult soul ever has the right to sexually abuse another soul—especially the young

No soul has the right to take another off of their life path

The Tools Available to Learn About Oneself

These can all be used positively or negatively.

Alchemy

Astrology

Herbs

Guides

Music

Yoga

Ley Lines

Feng Shui (placement of things around us)

Reiki (laying on of hands)

Dreams

Prayer

Qi Gong (Chinese healing art)

Rosary beads

Mantras

Psychic awareness

Chanting

Oracles

I Ching (Chinese reading of yarrow stalks)

Groundhog

Good witches

Hypnosis

Palmistry

Crystals, stones, gems

Angels

Meditation

Aromatherapy

Augury (from potents, omens, fall of lots)

Crypto zoology

Iridology (health revealed through the eyes)

Auras

Color

Psychometry

Bible, Torah, Koran, Dead Sea Scrolls

Tea leaves

Intuition

Altars/shrines

Rune stones

Automatic writing

Magnets

Diviners

Handwriting Analysis

Tarot

Numerology

Channels, readers, psychics

Mystics

Telekinesis

Reflexology

Healing touch (Pranic Healing)

Acupressure/acupuncture

Visualization

The Arts

Phrenology

Computer

Your Higher Self

Massage

Candle Lighting

Dowsing

Timeline

B.C. ("Before Christ")
Energy decides to create
Experiment with shadowy forms
Pockets of tribes on planet Earth
3 million—600,000 B.C. Atlantis and Lemuria
The misuse of energies and the destruction of Atlantis
Karmic debt is recorded to right the use of misuse
120,000—75,000, Neanderthal Man
Development of the body to survive
Development of the mind to think and reason
Development of the emotions to balance the mind and body
Development of the spiritual self to remember who you are,
    and why you are in physical form

9000	The Stone Age—Egypt and Mesopotamia
3760	The first date on the Jewish calendar
3600	The Bronze Age—Asia
2700	The building of Egypt's pyramids
2700	Acupuncture and herbal medicine used in China
2500	The Iron Age—The Middle East
1900	Stonehenge Built
1650	Abraham's family led the twelve tribes of Israel
1379	Egypt worships the Sun god
1250	Moses was born
1029	Buddha born, Lumbini garden, Nepal. Died 949
1000	The Maya Culture in Central America
1000	David to Jerusalem
850	*Iliad* and *Odyssey* written by Homer in Greece

776	First Olympic games in Greece
753	City of Rome founded
551	Confucius born in Shantung, China. Died, 478
472	Athens playwright, Aeschlus, has a theatre
430	Greek Philosopher, Leucippus, says: "Every natural event has a natural cause."
429	Physician Hippocrates' oath and the beginning of scientific medicine
427	Plato born in Athens, Greece. Died, 347
404	60-70,000 is the population of Athens, Greece
170	The world's first paved streets in Rome
79	The coliseum in Rome is completed
45	Julius Caesar died
36	Anthony and Cleopatra died
7	The world population is 150 million
5	Jesus born in Bethlehem

A.D. (Anno Domini, Latin, "In the year of the Lord," a time division in the Christian era)

20	Jesus visits the birthplace of Buddha in Nepal
27	Baptism of Jesus by John the Baptist
30	Crucifixion of Jesus
58	Buddhism introduced to China
64	Fire destroys Rome; Christians blamed
79	Volcano destroys Pompeii
221	Wall of China being built
330	Constantinople (Turkey) capital of the Roman Empire
372	Buddhism introduced into Korea
380	Rome adopts Christianity

The Middle Ages (about 500 to 1500 A.D.)

476	End of the West Roman empire (Rome, Italy)

552	Buddhism introduced to Japan
570	Mohammad born in Mecca, Saudi Arabia. Died 632
1000	Norseman Leif Ericsson's ship in North America
1453	Fall of the East Roman empire (Constantinople, Turkey)
1456	Gutenberg prints the first Bible
1457	First book printed in color
1492	Christopher Columbus discovers a new world
	Martin Behaim, Germany builds the first globe
	The Jews expelled from Spain, refusing to be Christians
1498	Michelangelo begins the Pièta sculpture
	The first pawnshop opens in Nuremberg, Bavaria (Germany)
1505	The design of the new Saint Peter's in Rome began
1509	Henry the 8th becomes the King of England
1510	Copernicus lets out the news that the Earth circles the sun
1520	Martin Luther expelled from the Catholic Church
1523	The first insurance policies issued for ships in Florence, Italy
1534	Henry the 8th begins the Church of England
1539	The first printing press and new Bible version printed
1550	Spain at the peak of political and economic power until 1600
1589	The French use forks at court
1600	William Shakespeare writes *Hamlet*
1604	Galileo proves the law of gravity
1607	The first permanent English colony, Jamestown, in North America

1611	The first Presbyterian Church in Virginia
1619	The first slaves sold to Jamestown colonists by the Dutch
1623	Patent laws begin in England to protect inventors
1624	New Amsterdam, now New York City, colony established
1628	The building of the Taj Mahal in India began
1636	Rhode Island, the first colony to grant complete religious freedom
1689	The first public schools in Philadelphia
1695	A personal ad placed for a marriage partner
1714	Tea, the second favorite drink after chocolate in New England
	Fahrenheit invents the mercury thermometer
1722	Six Indian nations make a treaty with the Virginia Settlers
1723	Christianity banned in China
1757	The Marquis de Lafayette born in France. Died 1834
1769	Napoleon Bonaparte born in Ajaccio, Corsica. Died 1821
1770	Ludwig Van Beethoven born in Bonn, Germany. Died 1827
1776	U.S. Congress adopts the Declaration of Independence
1784	Benjamin Franklin invents bifocal eyeglasses
1790	The Industrial revolution begins in America
1803	Lewis and Clark explore lands West of the Mississippi River
1806	Noah Webster publishes a dictionary
1806	Carbon paper developed for copies
1809	The Pall Mall section of London lighted by gas
1821	The copper-zinc battery invented

1825   Cuvier suggests great catastrophes have altered
        the Earth causing the extinction of whole animal
        species
1828   Democratic Party in U.S. formed by Andrew
        Jackson, the first democratic President.
1832   Samuel F.B. Morse designs the electromagnetic
        telegraph
        Louisa May Alcott born in Pennsylvania. Died
        1888
1835   The Polka first danced in Prague, Czechoslovakia
1837   Victoria becomes Queen of Great Britain and
        Ireland
1839   The first photograph by John Draper
1840   In the last ten years, 600,000 immigrants moved
        to the U.S.
1843   The fax process developed in Scotland
1845   The potato crops fail in Ireland
1848   The first women's rights convention in New York
1849   The gold rush to California
1851   San Francisco burns
1854   Republican Party calls for abolishing slavery
1855   Australia becomes self-governing
1857   Charles Darwin writes theories of evolution and
        natural selection
1858   The mechanical washing machine invented
1859   Work begins on the Suez Canal
1860   Abraham Lincoln elected U.S. President
1861   Florence Nightingale begins the world's first
        nursing school
1862   The American Civil War began
1863   The first auto with an internal combustion engine
        made
1865   The American Civil War ends

1867	Maria Sklodowska Curie born, Warsaw, Poland. Died 1934
1868	The first typewriter
1869	Louisa May Alcott publishes the book *Little Women*
	Mohandas Gandhi born, Porbandar, India. Died 1948
1871	Opening of the Suez Canal
1875	The first Kentucky Derby Race
	The first radio
1876	Alexander Graham Bell invents the telephone
1879	Thomas Edison invents the electric light bulb
1880	The first Barnum and Bailey Circus; last in 1956
1881	The first motion picture in France
1893	Mao Zedong born in China. Died 1976
1895	X—Rays of the human body
1897	Marconi begins a wireless telegraph company
1899	Aspirin is considered modern medicine
1901	Otis elevators and Carrier air conditioning began
1903	Wright Brothers fly
1908	Henry Ford makes an $850 Model T car
1910	Mother Theresa born in India. Died 1997
1912	The ship *Titanic* sinks
1914	World War One Begins; ends in 1919
1918	Anwar Sadat born in Egypt. Died 1981
1920	Women win the right to vote in the U.S.A.
	Pope John Paul II (Karol Wojtyla) born in Poland
1921	Microwaves and the lie detector invented
1922	Judy Garland born (Frances Gumm) in Minnesota. Died, 1969
1923	The bulldozer invented and sound for motion pictures
1927	Charles Lindberg flies from New York to France

1928   Rubber and plastic development in Germany
        Mickey Mouse born
        Television begins broadcasting
1929   Anne Frank born in Germany. Died 1945
        Martin Luther King born, Atlanta, Georgia. Died
        1968
1930   The first analog computer
1935   The Dalai Lama (the 12th) born in Taktser,
        Tibet
1938   The first toothbrushes made
1941   World War II begins; ends 1945
1944   The automatic calculator, a forerunner of digital
        computers
1945   Atomic Bomb explosion
1947   *The Diary of Anne Frank* published
        The Polaroid camera came into focus
1948   Transistors made
1950   The first organ transplant, one human to another
        The first commercial copier
1951   Sound and pictures on magnetic tape
        Electronic computer for commercial use devel-
        oped
1953   Color television developed
1954   Jonas Salk found anti-polio vaccine
1956   Air pollution is suggested to cause illness
1958   The first American satellite
1959   The first TV pictures of Earth from the "Explorer"
        Fidel Castro takes over Cuba
1960   Birth control pills
        John F. Kennedy elected president
        U.S. interest in Vietnam begins
        The working laser used
1961   Alan Shepard, the first man in space

The Berlin Wall separates East and West
Germany. Diana Spencer born in Great Britain.
Died 1997

1962 Computers in use
A mechanical heart used.

1963 John F. Kennedy assassinated

1964 Beatlemania
Awareness of land, air, and water pollution
Awareness of need to protect the animal kingdom

1965 U.S. air raids on Vietnam

1966 "Flower children" speak peace and love; East
beliefs come West

1967 Strides in medicines to help the mentally and
emotionally ill

1968 Martin Luther King assassinated

1969 Armstrong and Aldrin walk on the moon
The laser printer available for businesses
VCR recorders for home use
The computer network began

1970 World's population is 3.63 billion

1971 The first electronic (email) message

1972 End of the Vietnam conflict

1973 The first personal computers, France and U.S.
World's first computer internet connection

1975 The University of Southern California discovers a
new galaxy

1976 VHS, videocassette recorder

1977 Magnetic resonance image of the human body
Homosexual Human Rights law
The trans-Alaska pipeline system completed

1978 First test tube baby in England

1979 Mandatory retirement age to seventy years
The home video tape recorder
CDs (compact disc) player for sound by the Dutch
First cell phones in Tokyo, Japan

	CD-ROM of *Grolier's Encyclopedia*
1980	The international fax standard
1982	The camcorder
	First artificial heart in a man
1983	DNA genetic diagnosis
1988	The abortion pill
1989	Pro-democracy demonstrations in Beijing, China
1990	The Berlin Wall comes down
	Medicines of the East and West cultures are appreciated
	Greater technology to communicate all over the planet
	Politically correct thinking and behavior takes hold
1991	World's population is 5.5 billion
	The Soviet Union dissolved
1996	DVD released
1997	An energy shift towards wellness, wholeness, oneness
1999	A motion picture produced and exhibited with digital technology
2000	Old souls teaching younger souls the importance of self and the eternal creative energy of every soul on the Earth planet
	Age expectancy of man in modern world is 77 years
2001	Guide words for the new century: Spirituality

Tolerance of everyone's choices. Recognizing the best in everyone. Knowing you were like the worst person you know at one time. Being kind to everyone in all their stages of growth.

Forgiveness with compassionate understanding. Judging not, loving lots.

Bibliography

Even Angels have to give credit where credit is due. I wouldn't want to misuse another's energy. I thank all the soul energies that have written the following for all of us.

The Bible (And all its contributing writers and translators down through time.)

Bowker, John, ed. *The Oxford Dictionary of World Religions.* Oxford: Oxford University Press, 1997.

Byers, Paula Kay and Suzanne Michele Bourgoin. *Encyclopedia of World Biography.* Farmington Hills, MI: Gale Group, 1998.

Cooke, Jean, Ann Kramer, and Theodore Rowland-Entwistle, eds. History's Timeline. New York: Crescent Books, 1981.

Davis, Kenneth C. *Don't Know Much About the Bible.* New York: Harper Collins, 1998.

Holland, Barbara. "You Can't Keep A Good Prophet Down." *Smithsonian,* April 1999: 69-80.

The Keepers of the *Akashic Records* (at Home).

The Koran (Qur'an).